# LESSONS FROM LINDEN HILL

JERRY FRITZ
WITH
NANCY ONDRA

## DESIGN TIPS AND PLANNING POINTERS

Rick,
I hope you enjoy our lessons, Isn't it
a wonderful job we have to create
beautiful gardens for people to enjoy
Best
Jerry

ISBN: 1-4486-2677-3
EAN: 978-1-4486-2677-9

Printed in the United States of America by
CreateSpace

To purchase additional copies of this book, please
visit CreateSpace (www.createspace.com), Amazon
(www.amazon.com), or Linden Hill Gardens (www.
lindenhillgardens.com).

Linden Hill Gardens
P.O. Box 10
Ottsville, PA  18942
www.lindenhillgardens.com
610-847-1300

*To my wife, Amy, and our beautiful family: Clayton, Evan, Reid, and Lily. How can I start to thank a wife that is every man's dream? I cannot thank you enough for your constant guidance and strength in growing our family and business. I will never forget the first day I looked into your beautiful eyes. I would be lost without you. Thank you for all, Amy.*

*I look forward to a new lifelong lesson: to enjoy you and our family with all of my love.*

Jerry

# ACKNOWLEDGMENTS

After being in business for 20 years I have many people to thank. Without all of these people, my business would not have grown and allowed me to develop Linden Hill Gardens from a childhood dream to reality. I can remember drawing plans when I was a young boy, showing my mother what I wanted to do when I grew up.

My love and appreciation to my mother, Elizabeth Byrne, who worked so hard to raise me and taught me to be passionate in what I do and never compromise for second place. I will always remember what you did for me and know I will always love you.

My love and respect to my father, Jerry Fritz, who instilled in me a work ethic (I won't soon forget those 5 a,m, wakeup calls). He taught me to garden one way, the old-fashioned way — no shortcuts.

My admiration to Aunt Pat, who has always believed in me and has been a constant in my life. Thank you with all my might.

My sincere thanks to Delaware Valley College in Doylestown, PA, for employing two of the finest professors: David Benner, a gentleman with a heart of gold, and Rick Ray, with his dedication and his invitations for me to tag along on horticultural road trips.

The Perennial Plant Association is the finest group of fellow plant enthusiasts which have become my extended family. I thank all of the vendors who have grown and supplied me for years, with special thanks to Kim Bechtle at Still Pond Nursery, who has provided us so loyally but most important has become a dear friend.

My appreciation to all of my loyal clients who have allowed me and my staff to create beautiful gardens.

To my customers who have supported Linden Hill Gardens from the beginning, including Betsy McGrath, Jerry Abeles, Donna Berger, and countless others. I am so grateful for your loyalty and even more for our growing friendship.

To my awesome staff at Linden Hill for always going the extra mile: Matt Yoder, Jessica Myers, Marcos Gomez, Megan Crouthamel, and all of my Palisades High School Pirates.

To my friend and trusting confidant Peter Dubose who has guided me so many times over the years.

To Stephanie Cohen, who has always been able to help us promote new perennials in her cunning way.

My gratitude to my best friend Dan Heims of Terra Nova Nursery in Oregon who has always been there to listen and often advise. I will never forget meeting Dan in Vancouver and him asking me if I would like to see his heuchera leaves — the rest is history.

To Tasha Tudor for sharing her enchanting garden with me and my sons.

To Kristin Perry, whose talent and dedication is unmatched. I look forward to watching our gardens grow together as well as our friendship.

To my best friend Lynn Cohen who has more passion for perennials than anyone I know. I will always cherish our trips through New England.

Many thanks to Martha Stewart and her staff, who invited me on her television show and promoted my book even before it was printed. You have supported so many people over the years, my hat goes off to you.

To my in-laws, Doris and Bill Clayton, who have always been there for me and my family from the beginning, offering me my first location for our business. Bill has crafted so many wonderful buildings and is a true master craftsman but mostly a gentle giant with a beautiful soul. Thank you, Mom and Dad, for everything.

With all my love and true appreciation to my wife Amy and my children: Clayton, Evan, Reid (who I predict will be the next budding horticulturist), ; and Lily, who is my little princess. Thank you for your patience and dedication to my passion (did I say I'll be a bit late for dinner tonight?). You are my rock and I will always be there for you.

Well, I saved the best for last. I met Nancy Ondra at college and over the last few years asked if she would help me when I wrote my first book. Last year, after being in the hospital for nearly a week, I called Nancy and not only did she agree to help me start the book, she joined me in creating beautiful gardens at Linden Hill Gardens. Her knowledge and love of plants is unmatched in horticulture. I am so fortunate to have worked with Nancy on this book but mostly I feel from my heart that I have germinated a lifelong friendship that is most dear to me.

# CONTENTS

# PART ONE
## THE GARDENS AT LINDEN HILL

The Barn in 2000

The Barn in 2008

# CHAPTER 1

# LINDEN HILL: THE BEGINNING

So read the rustic sign that began the adventure known as Linden Hill Gardens, the culmination of my life-long dream to create an amazing horticultural destination. On the freezing February day that I drove by that sign back in 2000, I saw a nursery filled with all kinds of rare and unusual plants, complemented by extensive display plantings and packed with visitors who had come to learn about new plants and enjoy the glorious gardens. Well, that's what I saw in my imagination, at least. The reality was a little different.

Located in Bucks County, Pennsylvania, the property had a long history as a farm and homestead. Its agricultural heritage wasn't much in evidence on my first visit, though. For the last 25 years, it had been used as a dumping ground for all kinds of junk: old cars, trailers, broken machinery, and other debris. There were also several outbuildings, including a pig barn, horse barn, carriage barn, and smokehouse, all in various states of disrepair. The house, too, was filled with junk and habitable only for birds and mice. Then there was the main feature of the property (and the real prize, in my eyes): the big stone barn. A good part of its roof was missing, and the entire structure needed complete restoration. More than one friend told me I was crazy to consider taking it on. But, I like a challenge!

## JUST THE FACTS

As eager as I was to make the property mine and get started, I knew I needed to gather some solid facts about the place to back up my instincts. I wasn't new to the horticultural business, by any means. I'd started my landscaping business back in 1989 with just myself and a small pickup truck, and in just 11 years, I'd built it into a well-known and successful landscape design and installation firm, Jerry Fritz Garden Design, Inc. My wife, Amy, and I agreed that it was time to move the business to a separate location from our home, to have more room and peace for our growing family, and we had decided that a piece of commercial real estate would be a good investment.

**August 2000.** The barn didn't look too promising at this point, but the walls, at least, were sound.

My Aunt Pat, a successful Realtor, had drummed into me the mantra "Location, location, location," so I knew I had to look beyond the barn and land and seriously consider the property's prospects as a retail site. I figured that its placement on a seemingly busy main road was a plus, and to confirm that, I visited the property a half a dozen times to observe the passing traffic at various times of day, on both weekdays and weekends. As a further check, I contacted the state Department of Transportation to get their numbers for the estimated daily traffic on the road. What I saw confirmed that the property was high visibility, with plenty of potential customers passing by. I factored in the proximity of the site to New York City – it was less than 100 miles away – and felt sure that it could draw visitors from outside the immediate area as well as plenty of local traffic.

Then, there was the final piece of the puzzle: Would the site be suitable from a gardening perspective? I got the owner's permission to dig several test holes, and to my surprise – because this area is notorious from some very stony soils – I could easily dig down 5 feet without hitting a rock. I knew this was the perfect site for the display gardens I had in mind. Six months, twenty-one meetings, and seemingly endless negotiations later, the property was ours.

The very first day, my sons Clayton and Evan had fun exploring the barn and swinging from a rope fastened to one of the beams. That didn't last long, though: I offered to pay them each $1 for every bucket of trash they gathered. We all got busy, and we've been busy ever since.

**September 2000.** Once the debris was cleared away, restoration began with replacing the roof.

## DREAMS TO REALITY

I had big plans for developing this neglected property, based on other gardens and nurseries I had visited or read about as well as ideas of my own. I wanted it to feel a little like England, a little like Vermont, a little like the Hamptons, and a whole lot like Bucks County. A tall order, perhaps, but I knew I could do it.

One of the first steps was choosing a name for the property. I'd been excited to find several linden *(Tilia)* trees as I was exploring the wooded part of the acreage, because they don't commonly grow wild in the vicinity, so "Linden" seemed a perfect association for the uniqueness of the place. And while the property itself is relatively flat, it's located atop a ridge, so "Hill" seemed appropriate. "Nursery" might have been a more obvious choice to finish off the name, but I decided on "Gardens" instead. To my mind, the continually changing plantings here would be just as important as the exciting retail offerings in drawing people to return each year.

With the help of some local expertise and the design-build part of my own business, Linden Hill Gardens started to take shape. Excavator Fritz Bachman's team cut in the roads and parking lots and demolished most of the decaying buildings, except for one salvageable structure that we moved and converted into our office with the handiwork of master carpenter Bill Clayton. I hired local barn experts Curtis and Judy Iden and Brian Murphy to work on the restoration of the big barn, a process that ended up taking eight years from start to finish.

In between jobs for our design clients, our landscape crews began to develop some of the plantings and key features. We transplanted 50 large red cedars to provide screening from the neighbor's property to the north, and installed an earthen pond in a lower spot to gather runoff and eventually provide a place to showcase water-loving plants. Finally, we were ready to start

**November 2000.** A festive tent and seasonal plant groupings marked the site of our first Plant Event.

on the display gardens, beginning with the beds around the parking areas to welcome visitors and visually separate the retail sales area from the parking and storage areas needed by our landscape division. Each year since, we've developed one or more new garden areas, sometimes to serve equally practical purposes and sometimes just to add beauty or to experiment with design concepts (and sometimes for all three reasons).

The very first Linden Hill Gardens plant event was held in November of 2000, in a rented tent. We welcomed many old friends to our new space, and we also met many of our new neighbors, who were understandably curious about the many changes they saw going on here. Over the years, we've continued to develop our sales area, and we've expanded our schedule to include well over a dozen special event weekends, but we still aim to keep the spirit of freshness and excitement that made our very first event so memorable. I hope our visitors too will enjoy the mix of past, present, and future, as we continue to restore the glory of this beautiful farmstead and enhance it with extensive, ever-changing plantings for the enjoyment of other passionate gardeners.

# CHAPTER 2

# THE PARKING-LOT BEDS

The plantings at Linden Hill Gardens started in fall of 2000 in a central location, linking the main entrance of the property to the retail entrance and creating an attractive parking area for our customers. At a loss for a more clever name, we call them the Parking-Lot Beds.

## BEHIND THE DESIGN

The upper (northernmost) Parking-Lot Bed divides the retail parking site from the longer driveway that leads back to the landscape business area, and the lower one separates the retail parking from the office parking. I wanted them to be more than just space-fillers, though. I envisioned a grand display of color and texture to welcome our visitors, with plenty of seasonal changes to entice them to return again and again, and the beds serve that purpose perfectly. From bark and berries for winter through bulbs and wildflowers for spring, blooming annuals and perennials for summer, and glorious seedheads and foliage for fall, there's always something to look at! The Parking-Lot Beds seem especially popular with our customers in July and August, a time when many gardeners are looking for ways to make their own gardens look good through the sultry summer months.

**The layered look.** Both of these free-form planting areas fit the definition of an island bed, because they're visible from all sides. The traditional design approach to island beds is to place the tallest plants in the middle, tapering to the smallest along the edges, and I followed that

to some extent. But I also like to bring some taller plants closer to the edge in some places, to break up the layers a bit and create smaller niches where we can highlight different plant combinations. This encourages visitors to walk around the entire perimeter of each bed, since they can't see the whole thing at once.

**Raising the roots.** The site where the Parking-Lot Beds are located is quite flat, so I decided to raise the grade there, mounding the soil to about 3 feet toward the middle of each planting area and tapering it down to ground level around the edges. The change in elevation adds a lot of visual interest, and it helps to emphasize the feeling of enclosure where the beds wrap around the parking area. The slight slope makes it a little easier to see the individual plants, as well. And on a purely practical level, berming up the beds raised the surface of the planting areas above the grade of the sometimes-soggy ground there, providing ideal rooting conditions for a wide range of plants.

**Pass-through paths.** The two Parking-Lot Beds are both long and wide, so it made sense to add several pathways through them. Built from large fieldstones, the paths entice visitors to walk through the beds as well as around them. Where one of the paths winds through the widest part of the lower bed, there's even room for a garden bench that's otherwise hidden from view, creating the feeling of a private garden room in the midst of an otherwise high-traffic area.

**A shady retreat.** Tucked into a shady spot within the lower Parking-Lot Bed, this forget-me-not blue bench provides an unexpected splash of color.

These paths create plenty of exciting planting opportunities, too. We've tucked a number of different perennial ground covers between and around the stones, including creeping mazus (*Mazus reptans*), blue star creeper (*Laurentia fluviatilis*), and low-growing thymes (*Thymus*) and sedums (*Sedum*). It's also been interesting to observe which plants move themselves into these pathways, such as the purple-leaved Labrador violet (*Viola labradorica*). Our visitors can see for themselves how these various groundcovers perform in our area and how they respond to occasionally being stepped on — something you can't guess just by looking at the plants in a pot or picture.

**Along the edge.** Except for where the space is too limited, the perimeter of the Parking-Lot Beds is surrounded by a 6-foot-wide band of turfgrass. Keeping it mowed and edged adds some maintenance time, but I wouldn't be without it. The rich green grass creates a beautiful setting for the more colorful plantings, and it also provides a much-needed buffer zone between the cars and the plants.

## PICKING THE PLANTS

Even though the nursery is currently open only from April through October, we have friends and clients stopping by all year 'round, so four-season interest was a must. That, along with the large size of the beds (which allowed for a few good-sized trees), made a mixed planting of woody and herbaceous plants an obvious choice.

**Starting with structure.** To get immediate height and screening — and to create some much-needed shade as well — we started with a backbone of deciduous and evergreen trees: several 'Green Giant' arborvitaes (*Thuja*), Persian ironwoods (*Parrotia persica*), and Japanese tree lilacs (*Syringa reticulata*), as well as a large nannyberry (*Viburnum prunifolium*) and a 'Winter King' hawthorn (*Crataegus viridis*). Some key shrubs that make up the middle layer in the Parking-Lot Beds include 'Cameo' flowering quince (*Chaenomeles* x *superba*) for early spring blossoms; bottlebrush buckeye (*Aesculus parviflora*) for midsummer bloom and yellow fall color; Knock Out rose (*Rosa* 'Radrazz') for flowers from early summer to mid-fall; and 'Dart's Gold' ninebark (*Physocarpus opulifolius*) for spring through fall foliage interest, early summer flowers, midsummer seed capsules, and handsome bark for winter.

**Mixing it up.** The ground layer of herbaceous plants changes often as we replace older cultivars with new introductions to keep things fresh. Seeing the "latest and greatest" cultivars actually growing in the ground helps both us and our customers judge how the plants look in real-life conditions, which is sometimes very different from what we expected from the catalog descriptions or pot tags. Star performers get plenty of attention; disappointments get transplanted or composted. We also use these display beds to try out new combinations of older favorites. When our visitors see plant pairings that perform well for us, they're often inspired to recreate the same or similar combinations in their own gardens.

## OVER THE YEARS

Our habit of replacing annuals and moving perennials around frequently is a surprise to some of our customers, though many have come to expect seeing new plants and combinations each time they stop by. One thing that can shock even our regulars, though, is our willingness to move even the large woody plants. Along comes a nursery customer looking to buy a full-sized shrub or a landscape client needing a special tree, and away goes a big part of a bed's structure! But we're pleased to provide this special service for fellow gardeners, and we always enjoy having the

opportunity to try something completely different in an empty spot.

Every time any plant gets moved out of the beds, we enrich the empty spot with a mixture of well-rotted cow manure (to help maintain the soil fertility) and perlite (to help keep the soil loose). And once a year, usually in early summer, we top-dress both beds with a slow-release organic fertilizer and cover the soil with a shredded leaf mulch, to maintain the health and fertility of the beds as a whole.

Nearly a decade after their installation, the Parking-Lot Beds are still doing a great job serving every purpose I'd originally envisioned for them. I like them so much, in fact, that I'm thinking of expanding them so they meet in the middle, which will allow even more planting options and provide yet another place to include a meandering stepping-stone path. Gardens sure have a way of growing on us, don't they?

**A colorful welcome.** The mixed plantings in the Parking-Lot Beds provide months of color and textural interest.

# Lessons from the Parking-Lot Beds

While the Parking-Lot Beds at Linden Hill are more extensive than most home landscapes have space for, they offer plenty of pointers that are suitable for any garden space.

***Solutions for salt.*** Plantings around parking areas and walkways face a special challenge in cold climates: the salt used to melt ice in winter. This is especially a problem for beds that are slightly below grade, so that they catch any salt-laden runoff. Building up the surface of the bed even just a few inches above the sur-

**On the edge.** Leaving a strip of turf around a bed adds some extra maintenance, in the form of mowing and edging. But it's worth the effort, because it creates a beautiful frame for the plantings, and it provides a buffer from vehicles, too.

rounding soil can go a long way to preventing damage to your plants later on. Or, use sand instead to provide traction, then sweep it into the beds in spring.

***Where will the snow go?*** Snow, too, can be a problem if you don't plan for it when you design plantings around parking areas. When it's time to remove that snow, you need a place to put it! It's fine to pile plenty of snow on dormant perennials; in fact, it makes a great winter mulch. Woody plants, though, can be damaged by the impact of heavy snow

**Where will the snow go?** If winter snows tend to be heavy where you live, plan ahead for space to put what you shovel or plow. Planting annuals and perennials along the edge of the border provides plenty of space for piling snow without damaging the shrubs.

height and seasonal interest. It's tempting to set these youngsters fairly close together for immediate impact, but that can create crowding problems later on. Do your homework before planting so you allow plenty of space for each one to reach its mature size. Or, consider shrubs and trees that don't mind being pruned heavily, so you can whack them back to a 1- to 3-foot framework in early to mid-spring if they get too big. Some woody plants that can tolerate this treatment include butterfly bushes (*Buddleia*), catalpa (*Catalpa bignonioides*), elderberries (*Sambucus*), shrubby dogwoods (*Cornus*), shrub-type willows (*Salix*), and smoke bushes (*Cotinus*).

thrown from a snow-blower or by the force of snow piles pushed by a plow. Keeping a strip of grass at least 2 feet — and ideally about 6 feet — wide can prevent most of these problems.

***Avoid watering woes.*** Raised beds are ideal for expanding your planting options in sites that tend to be too wet for most plants, or that are too rocky to dig easily. Just keep in mind that the bermed soil can dry out more quickly than you expect. Our beds are in a very windy site, so we ended up installing an underground irrigation system. You may want to consider that during the design process for your own beds, or else be prepared to have to hand-water during dry spells.

***Consider cut-backs.*** Unless you're creating new mixed plantings around established shrubs or trees, you'll probably be planting at least a few young woodies for

**A bright idea.** Hard pruning in spring encourages lots of bright new growth on purple-leaved smoke bushes (*Cotinus*), such as 'Royal Purple'.

CHAPTER 3

# THE LONG BORDER

When it was time to think about a site for Linden Hill's second display garden, putting it along our road frontage seemed an obvious choice. After all, nearly 30,000 cars pass by here every day, and what better way to lure in the gardeners than a beautiful planting? An eye-catching border in this high-visibility site would also be excellent advertising to attract potential landscape clients. The Long Border has served both of those purposes admirably, and it's become something of a neighborhood landmark as well.

## BEHIND THE DESIGN
I knew that I wanted to install a wooden post-and-rail fence as the backdrop for the planting, because it would perfectly suit the farm-like feel of the property, and of Bucks County in general. Deciding what to put in front of it was more of a challenge.

I had plenty of irises, peonies, and daylilies (*Hemerocallis*) on hand, so I first considered a narrow row of these combined with my signature plant, catmint (*Nepeta*). Before I committed to that, though, I decided I'd better look at the site as a potential customer would see it. I drove past it a number of times at varying speeds and began to think that large drifts of plants would be a more attention-grabbing option, but I was still undecided. My friend Lynn Cohen happened to be in town around that time, and when I told her about my mass-planting idea, her immediate

response was "Fritzie, that's boring! That's not your look. Why don't you lay it out like you were a planning a client's garden?" I decided that she was absolutely right, and so began the Long Border.

**Sizing up the site.** When I say Long Border, I *mean* long: the site I wanted to plant measured 300 feet from end to end. Now, how wide to make it? I started thinking 8 feet, but Lynn and I agreed it needed to be deeper, so it became 10 feet, then 12, then 15, then 20, and finally 22 feet. To check our decision, I placed a 6-foot-tall oak stake at each end of the space and ran a string line between the two, about 3 feet off the ground, so I could get a better idea of the proportions we were considering. After a night spent dreaming about all the exciting combinations I could create in this new garden, I walked out to the site, looked again at the staked-out space, and knew the length and depth of the border-to-be were perfect.

**Getting rid of the grass.** Anyone who has built a garden knows how daunting it can be to look at an expanse of turfgrass and try to figure out how to remove it. Hand-digging over 6000 square feet of sod simply wasn't an option, and even using a gas-powered sod cutter would have taken an enormous amount of labor. I didn't want to use herbicide, either. So, I decided to do what the experts always tell you *not* to do: dig the existing turf into the soil. That led me to yet another dilemma: Even a large rotary tiller

19

FALL
2001

JULY
2008

couldn't handle a job this tough, so what kind of equipment did I need? This time, good advice came from my neighbor Joe Fleck, who recommended having local farmer Clarence Berger come out and chisel-plow the site. Well, big borders call for big equipment, and sure enough, the plow did a super job at turning under that sod and breaking up the compacted clay.

**Building up the soil.** As eager as I was to get busy planting, I wanted to take the extra step of preparing the best possible rooting conditions for our new border. Luckily, I had plenty of organic matter on hand, in the form of a huge pile of compost we'd made using the garden debris from Linden Hill as well as our clients' properties. Excavator Doug Pannapacker made quick work of hauling approximately 30 dump-truck loads of compost from the pile to the border and roughly leveling the site. We weren't finished yet, though! Our garden and landscape crews then spread over 100 large bags of coarse perlite and 80 cubic yards of leaf mold over the area, and tilled it all in. We gave the site some time to settle, and in October of 2001, we were finally ready to plant.

## PICKING THE PLANTS

Oh, the possibilities! To narrow the options a bit, I decided to go with a color scheme based on pastels and white, with touches of more intense hues.

**Starting with structure.** I frequently add woody plants to the gardens I create, because they provide height and seasonal interest even when the herbaceous plants have died off for the winter. I didn't want to go with a tree layer as we had in the Parking-Lot Beds, though, because I envisioned the Long Border staying a full-sun, color-rich space. So here, the backbone of the border came from medium-sized deciduous shrubs, including 'Royal Purple' smoke bush (*Cotinus coggygria*) for summer and fall foliage color; butterfly bushes (*Buddleia*), panicle hydrangeas (*Hydrangea paniculata*) for summer-into-fall flowers; *Viburnum nudum* 'Winterthur' for summer flowers, showy fall berries, and great autumn leaf color; and 'Winter Flame' dogwoods (*Cornus sanguinea*) for colorful cold-season stems.

**The summer spectacle.** The conical white bloom clusters of panicle hydrangea (*Hydrangea paniculata*) add eye-catching impact to the Long Border in August, complemented by touches of "blurple" from phlox and catmint (*Nepeta*) and pinks from dwarf cannas and 'Siskiyou' showy evening primrose (*Oenothera speciosa*).

**Autumn abundance.** As the season progresses, the Long Border's color theme gets more intense, with high-impact combinations such as Tiger Eyes sumac (*Rhus typhina* 'Bailtiger') and 'Gibraltar' bush clover (*Lespedeza thunbergii*).

**Mixing it up.** Tall-stemmed perennials such as compass plant (*Silphium perfoliatum*), 'Dallas Blues' switch grass (*Panicum virgatum*), giant coneflower (*Rudbeckia maxima*), Joe-Pye weed (*Eupatorium maculatum*), 'Lemon Queen' perennial sunflower (*Helianthus*), lavender mist meadow rue (*Thalictrum rochebruneanum*), and Tatarian aster (*Aster tataricus*) drift among the shrub groupings, supplying even more seasonal color and textural interest. I made sure to pick perennials that I knew were sturdy enough to stand up without support, because having to

stake the plants in a border that size would be a maintenance nightmare.

Closer to the middle of the border are a wide variety of medium-sized shrubs and perennials, among them dwarf arctic willow (*Salix purpurea* 'Nana') — which, at 6 to 8 feet tall, is anything *but* dwarf — Endless Summer hydrangea (*Hydrangea macrophylla* 'Bailmer'), Virginia sweetspire (*Itea virginica*), 'Hot Lips' pink turtlehead (*Chelone lyonii*), Mellow Yellow spirea (*Spiraea thunbergii* 'Ogon'), bluestars (*Amsonia*), 'Purple Smoke' false indigo (*Baptisia*), and variegated Japanese iris (*Iris ensata* 'Variegata'). All of these plants have proven themselves to be tough and trouble-free, so I knew I could count on them to provide a long season of interesting forms, flowers, and/or foliage with a minimum of fussing from us.

And finally, it was time to fill in the front of the border, primarily with more workhorse perennials in the range of 6 to 36 inches tall. Some star performers here include black-eyed Susan (*Rudbeckia fulgida*), 'Caradonna' perennial sage (*Salvia*), 'Raydon's Favorite' aromatic aster (*Aster oblongifolius*), 'Purple Emperor' sedum, Rozanne geranium (*Geranium* 'Gerwat'), 'Siskiyou' pink evening primrose (*Oenothera speciosa*), and 'Walker's Low' catmint (*Nepeta*).

## OVER THE YEARS

We had a few plant losses during the first winter due to a drainage problem, but we quickly fixed that by creating a swale along the back of the border to redirect some runoff water and by working some more perlite into the overly-moist area. Otherwise, nearly 10 years later, almost all of my original choices are still thriving in the Long Border.

That's not to say that we haven't made changes, of course. The plants grow quickly in the well-prepared soil, so we've removed quite a few over the years, either to relieve overcrowding or because we needed landscape-size plants for retail customers or design clients. In some cases, we've left the original plants but control their size by pruning them heavily in March — down to about 18 inches for the dwarf arctic willow and to about 3 feet for the smokebush — a technique called stooling. We've been digging out the compass plants too, because they self-sowed too freely and the seedlings were coming up throughout the planting area.

The color scheme of the Long Border has changed somewhat, as well. Linden Hill was going to host a big party in late July of 2008 as part of the Perennial Plant Association's annual conference, and I wanted the visitors' first glimpse of the property to be unforgettable. Our horticulturist, Nancy Ondra, wove chartreuse 'Margarita' and deep purple 'Sweet Caroline Purple' sweet potato vines (*Ipomoea batatas*), glowing 'Profusion Orange' zinnias, deep red 'Elephant's Head' amaranth, sunny yellow lantanas, and dozens of other annuals and tender perennials among the existing hardy perennials and shrubs to create the desired summer spectacle. Normally, I prefer quieter color schemes, but to my surprise, I loved the effect — and, judging by the compliments we received, our customers enjoyed it too.

We have yet another change in mind for the near future: the addition of bulbs for spring color. There's plenty of space available before the perennials and shrubs leaf out, and it's a shame not to make use of it. It'll take a whole lot of daffodils to make a great show, but we can already envision how spectacular it will look.

**Finishing touches.** In a large-scale planting, repeating groupings of similar colors and plant forms helps to visually tie the whole area together. But don't forget to add some dramatic accents, too. Strongly vertical 'Elephants Head' amaranth (*Amaranthus*) certainly grabbed lots of attention here in late summer.

# Lessons from the Long Border

Whether they're 60 square feet or over 6000, like our roadside planting at Linden Hill, borders are handy for many design situations. Unlike free-standing island beds, borders are generally tied into some vertical or horizontal element — a fence or wall, for instance, or a path or walkway — so they're handy for creating a transition between the hardscape and the landscape.

***Avoid the stair-step effect.*** Because borders are seen mostly from one side, it's natural to want to keep the tallest plants at the back, the shortest at the front, and the medium-sized ones in the middle. Don't stick to that too strictly, though. It's far more in- teresting if you bring a few taller plants toward the front to break up the layers a bit, and let the shorter ones weave into the middle layers. You can see that in the mid-June shot of the Long Border below, and even more in the mid-August view on the opposite page.

**Give them their space.** In a small border, you can get away with setting the perennials at fairly close spacings at planting time to get a more finished look right away. That's usually cost-prohibitive in a large border, though, from the perspective of needing many more plants as well as the labor involved in first planting them and then thinning them out or dividing them just a year or two later. It's far easier to space the perennials 18 to 24 inches apart at the beginning, then use inexpensive annuals such as coleus, compact zinnias, sweet potato vine (*Ipomoea batatas*), and verbenas as fillers for the first year.

**Think ahead about maintenance.** Unless you're planning a border that's no more than 2 or 3 feet wide, it's smart to think ahead about how you're going to reach all of the plants to care for them. At the very least, leave a 2- to 4-foot-wide mulched path along the back for easier access; you won't even see it from the front. And in very deep plantings, consider designing meandering paths into the border. That will make weeding, mulching, and other maintenance tasks much easier, and it will also invite visitors in to enjoy the plants and combinations up close.

CHAPTER 4

# THE OFFICE BORDERS

The center of activity at Linden Hill is our office, located in the heart of our retail sales space. My father-in-law, Bill Clayton, created the structure from the remains of an old pig barn, using other recycled materials he found on the property to produce a pleasingly rustic effect. In 2006, I finally got around to crafting a planting that would complement it.

## BEHIND THE DESIGN
I'm always in favor of gardens that are functional as well as beautiful, and this site seemed like a great opportunity to showcase an out-of-the-ordinary foundation planting that I could use to give our landscape-design clients ideas for their own properties. At the same time, I could work in yet another of those classic elements of a British garden — a double border — though on a somewhat smaller scale (35 feet long by 6 feet wide for each side).

The Linden Hill office sits in a flat, open area, with a living patio at the entrance. The planting runs along the northwest side of the building, facing the office parking area. Seen from that angle, it looks like a foundation planting that includes a mix of small trees, shrubs, and perennials. As you get closer to the office, though, you can see that the planting is actually two borders with a stepping-stone path running down the middle. That path originally led to an open lawn area; now it leads to our Gift Cottage and cottage garden. While the site gets sun all day long, the building casts some shade on the border right next to it, allowing us to showcase both shade and sun plants.

## PICKING THE PLANTS
Because the office is such a high-traffic area, and so is the path through the office borders, it was important to me to have something to look at throughout the year. I decided on a mixed planting, with everything from woody plants and vines down through herbaceous perennials, annuals, bulbs, and groundcovers. (You'd be amazed at how many plants I can pack into even a small space!) This is one of the gardens I get to see most often, even during our busiest season, so I elected to focus on one of my favorite pairings — blue and chartreuse — for the overall color theme.

**Starting with structure.** Yews (*Taxus*) or arborvitae (*Thuja*) planted in a straight line and sheared into cones, cubes, or globes are a common sight in foundation plantings our part of Pennsylvania, but *not* in the planting at Linden Hill, I assure you. Instead, our repetition comes from three sweetbay magnolias (*Magnolia virginiana*) and three 'Pink Diamond' hydrangeas (*Hydrangea paniculata*), which have the advantage over evergreens of offering changing interest through the seasons. And instead of being lined up in one narrow border along the building,

27

**Making scents.** Fragrant flowers and foliage add another leavel of pleasure to a beautiful border. Dwarf Korean lilac (*Syringa meyeri* 'Palibin') is one of my top picks for fragrance.

they zig-zag across the path (two magnolias and one hydrangea in the outer border; one magnolia and two hydrangeas in the other). From a distance, this gives the planting a richer, layered appearance, and up close, it enhances the feeling that you're walking through one garden instead of two separate plantings.

For variety, I added a few more deciduous shrubs, including a winter hazel (*Corylopsis*) for spring flowers; Golden Spirit smoke bush (*Cotinus coggygria* 'Ancot'), Mellow Yellow spirea (*Spiraea thunbergii* 'Ogon'), and Tiger Eyes sumac (*Rhus typhina* 'Bailtiger') for bright yellow foliage; and Endless Summer hydrangea (*Hydrangea macrophylla* 'Bailmer') for summer and fall flowers.

One more structural touch that looks good all year 'round is a granite hitching post at the end closest to the office door, where it helps to mark the entrance to the borders. It also serves as some support for a sprawling 'Mrs. Robert Brydon' clematis, which contributes fragrant, icy blue blooms to the planting in July and August.

**Mixing it up.** The golden-leaved shrubs add plenty of yellow to the borders, so I brought in a lot of blue and blurple (blue-purple) with the herbaceous plants. There's an abundance of irises, of course, including reblooming bearded hybrid 'Clarence', with light blue flowers, and later-blooming variegated Japanese iris (*Iris ensata* 'Variegata'), which is a rich purple. I also had to include another of my signature plants — 'Walker's Low' catmint (*Nepeta*) — mingled with Wlassov's geranium (*Geranium wlassovianum*) to serve as a groundcover under one of the magnolias. Creeping mazus (*Mazus reptans*) was another must-have for filling in around and between the stepping stones.

The far end of the borders tends to be very damp, giving us a chance to incorporate some lesser-used moisture-lovers, including fingerleaf rodgersia (*Rodgersia aesculifolia*) and umbrella plant (*Darmera peltata*). Some other herbaceous highlights include more yellow-leaved plants, among them bold 'Sun Power' hosta, aromatic golden oregano (*Origanum vulgare* 'Aureum'), ever-gold 'Angelina' sedum (*Sedum rupestre* 'Angelina'), and spiky 'All Gold' Japanese wind grass (*Hakonechloa macra*).

Not one to miss any available planting space, I decided to do some vertical gardening too. At the middle and far end of the office shed wall, a climbing hydrangea (*Hydrangea anomala* subsp. *petiolaris*) has settled in well, and I can't wait until it's mature enough to start producing its lacy white flower clusters.

## OVER THE YEARS

With so many of us walking through these borders every day, you can bet that any bare spots that appear don't stay bare for long before someone — quite often, our retail manager, Jessica Myers — fills them with more plants. For early color, we pack any empty spaces we can find with sky blue forget-me-nots (*Myosotis*) and purple and blue violas (especially my favorite 'Yesterday, Today and Tomorrow'). When the heat causes them to fizzle out in early to midsummer, we replace them with angelonias, mini-petunias, and verbenas in the same color range. We've also been experimenting with some dark-leaved annuals, including 'Bull's Blood' beets and 'Merlot' lettuce.

Last fall, we tucked many spring ephemerals around the base of the shrubs and larger perennials. Trilliums, Canada mayflowers (*Maianthemum canadense*), and spring beauties (*Claytonia virginica*) will have plenty of time to pop up, bloom, and then go dormant again before their taller companions leaf out enough to cover them. And for late-season color, we added masses of fall-flowering crocus and colchicums under each of the sweetbay magnolias. The open branching habit of the trees provides just enough shade to keep the flowers from getting scorched but still gives them plenty of sunlight to ripen their strappy spring foliage.

**Growing up.** When planning a border along a building, don't forget to take advantage of the wall for planting. In one of our Office Borders, climbing hydrangeas (*Hydrangea anomala* subsp. *petiolaris*) is slowly creeping up the wall, providing a pretty background for the abundance of golden foliage.

# Lessons from the Office Borders

There's something magical about being able to walk *through* a garden instead of just look at it. A planted pathway to your front door creates a friendly, welcoming feel, and a flower- and fragrance-filled route between your house and car gives a quick recharge to your spirits as you head out and back. When you can create a planting that does all of that *and* gives your home outstanding curb appeal, why would you ever stick with a traditional foundation planting of boring evergreens?

***Let loose your inner artist.*** When you're planting next to a building, don't overlook the possibilities of creating some exciting color effects with the paint and the plants. I chose a dark green paint for the exterior of the Linden Hill office, for example, because I could envision it making an excellent backdrop for both the chartreuse foliage and the blue flowers. But I wasn't finished there: I took a leaf of the chartreuse 'Margarita' sweet potato vine (*Ipomoea batatas*) to a local paint store for them to match and used that color for the building's window trim. It was a perfect echo for the many golden-leaved

plants in the garden and really completed the scene.

***Keep them close.*** A planted pathway like this is a perfect place to show off small specimens of extra-special perennials. You can easily watch their progress as you walk by them often, making sure that they get the pampering they need and preventing them from getting crowded out by bigger companions. Once the little gems have matured enough to hold their own, you can move them to other parts of your garden.

***Don't skimp on the width.*** It's nice to be able to brush against some plants as you stroll along a garden path, but if it gets too overgrown, it can be difficult or even dangerous to walk through. You can save yourself a lot of cutting-back later if you make the path plenty wide at the very beginning. In a light-traffic area — a walkway leading to a side or back door, for example — you can get away with a planted path that's 24 to 30 inches wide. A heavily traveled path really needs to be wider: 3 to 4 feet across is usually about right.

**Crafting a path (above).** A 3- to 4-foot-wide walkway may look *too* wide at first, but trust me: once the plants start filling in, it will be just right.

**Color your world (opposite).** Matching trim colors to plants (or vice versa) is one of those designer touches that makes even a simple border picture perfect.

# CHAPTER 5

# THE LIVING PATIO

What in the world is a living patio? Let me tell you the story behind the idea, and it'll make perfect sense. About 20 years ago, I was working on an extensive design for a client just outside Philadelphia, and part of that included creating an outdoor sitting area. Since the entire design had a naturalistic feel, a formal terrace would have looked out of place, so I suggested paving the area with natural fieldstone instead, with gaps left between the stones for plants to grow in. The client liked the idea, and so the stones were soon laid, and I set a sprinkler in the middle of the area to soak the soil well to prepare it for planting.

When we arrived the next day to finish the job, the next-door neighbor (who had been observing our progress from her kitchen window) walked over soon after, greeting us with a bemused "Now I've seen everything! You're crazy to water a patio." I explained that we were going to plant in it, and she thought I was kidding and laughed. Well, I had my turn to chuckle when that neighbor called our office less than a year later to ask us to install a "living patio" for her too. The name stuck, and these two installations were just the first of many living patios that I've designed and planted since then, including one right outside our office at Linden Hill.

## BEHIND THE DESIGN

Our office is the center of operations for both Linden Hill Gardens and Jerry Fritz Garden Design, so it's a busy place with both staff and clients coming and going. The high-traffic entrance needed some kind of sturdy footing, but I wanted it to look good too, so a living patio was an ideal solution. It adds a welcoming touch to our base of operations, it provides a new place for us to trial various plants, and it's a handy visual aid when potential clients come to discuss their projects. Instead of telling them what a living patio looks like, I can simply open the door and show them.

**Selecting the stones.** The stones are the heart of any living patio. This isn't the place to use up small pieces, because they won't stay level, and that can cause people to trip; plus, the whole effect looks "busy." I prefer to use large, flat slabs of Pennsylvania fieldstone, ranging in size from 3 to 10 feet wide and 4 to 8 inches thick.

The colors range from dusty olive to rusty brown, and the surfaces are often marked with ripples or tiny pockets. I like to include a few of the stones with pockets or shallow indentations in each patio, because they collect water that birds can easily drink from or bathe in. That makes living patios wildlife-friendly as well as people- and plant-friendly. Come to think of it, they're environmentally friendly too: instead of rainfall sheeting off the solid surface of a formally paved patio, it can soak into the ground through the spaces between the stones, reducing the overall water runoff from a property.

**Amazing mazus.** The ground cover known as creeping mazus (*Mazus reptans*) is one of my favorite choices for filling in and around living patios and stone walkways. Even when it's not in bloom, it creates a handsome carpet of green that complements colorful companions.

**Proper patio prep.** I approached the Linden Hill living patio project in the same way I recommend to my clients: I guessed at the dimensions I wanted, and then outlined the space on the ground with marking paint. I set out the kind of furniture and accessories I planned to keep on the patio (in this case, a two-person garden bench and a decorative pot), then lived with the space for a week or two.

Once I knew the proportions were right, it was time to excavate. I like to use at least 6 to 8 inches of 3/4-inch modified crushed stone as a base for living patios, so we dug out the area to a depth of about 1 foot. That allowed for the crushed stone and the varying thicknesses of the stone slabs to make the final surface of our patio about 2 inches above the surrounding grade. A living patio doesn't normally *have* to be raised; I just decided to do that to avoid adding a step up into the office.

I'll add here that it's never a bad idea to lay a 1-inch conduit pipe into the gravel bed for a living patio, in case you need to run and electrical or irrigation line through the area in the future. The cost of adding it at this stage is negligible compared to having to dig up those big stone slabs later!

**Setting the stones.** Once the crushed-stone base was tamped and then sprinkler-watered overnight to prevent further settling, it was time to place the slabs. Moving stones this size requires heavy equipment, such as a small front-end loader or backhoe. Other tools I find useful are a 4-foot hand level for making sure that the stones are flat and a sturdy, 5-foot metal digging bar for shifting them around. Finding the perfect placement for each stone is much like putting together a jigsaw puzzle. I try to leave a space about 1 inch wide between each of the stones as I arrange them. Their edges are naturally irregular, though, so there are plenty of larger gaps that create planting pockets.

Once we'd filled between the stone slabs of our living patio with a homemade "grouting mixture (equal parts of topsoil, coarse sand, and stone screenings), we swept off the excess, watered the area thoroughly to settle the grouting mix, and we were ready to plant.

## PICKING THE PLANTS

Some perennial growers have coined names like Jeepers Creepers or Stepables for their lines of ground covers, and they divide them into groups based on how well they tolerate being walked on. I didn't stick with one particular "brand" or group, though, because I wanted to trial a wide variety of plants and judge their performance for myself.

My only guideline was to stick with plants that reached a maximum of about 8 inches in bloom and 2 to 3 inches tall in leaf, which narrowed down my options somewhat, but it still gave me many dozens of species and cultivars to try. Some, such as purple-leaved Labrador violet (*Viola labradorica*) were mostly for foliage color; others, including the veronicas, are primarily there for pretty flowers. We also tucked in low-growing thymes (*Thymus*) and other herbs with scented foliage, because they release a nice fragrance when they get stepped on.

## OVER THE YEARS

The Linden Hill patio gets baked in the sun from dawn until late afternoon for most of the year, so it gets pretty hot out there. And while it does receive an occasional sprinkling as we're hand-watering the plantings next to it, we rarely make a point of watering the paver plants once they've been in place for a few weeks. It's hardly surprising, then, that not all of our choices have been equally happy in this site. A few that eventually died out included purple-leaved sea thrift (*Armeria maritima* 'Rubrifolia'), woolly thyme (*Thymus pseudolanuginosus*), and white-flowered creeping mazus (*Mazus reptans* 'Albus'), which seems touchier than the straight species. These minor losses are no problem, though, because they give us an opportunity to try something else in those spots. After a few seasons, some star performers have become evident:

- **In the main part of the patio (a high-traffic area):** Creeping mazus (*Mazus reptans*), creeping thyme (*Thymus serpyllum*), elfin thyme (*T. serpyllum* 'Minus'), goldmoss sedum (*Sedum acre*), Roman chamomile (*Chamaemelum nobile*), and Scotch moss (*Sagina subulata* 'Aurea').

- **Around the edges of the patio (where the plants seldom get stepped on):** 'Aztec Gold', 'Georgia Blue' and 'Waterperry Blue' veronica (*Veronica*), Chocolate Chip ajuga (*Ajuga reptans* 'Valfredda'), golden oregano (*Origanum vulgare* 'Aureum'), and Labrador violet (*Viola labradorica*).

One plant that doesn't always make it through the winter is Corsican mint (*Mentha requienii*), but I don't mind popping in a few more pieces each spring because I love it so much. Its bright green leaves are tiny, but their minty scent is so intense when you rub or step on them that I consider it a must-have for living patios!

While the successful plants have done a great job filling in the gaps between the stones, we occasionally have a few bare spots. Sometimes, we simply transplant pieces of the good spreaders into those spaces; other times, we use those gaps to try out new creepers. Like all of our other gardens, our living patio is constantly changing — for the better, of course!

**On the edge.** Glowing yellow 'Angelina' sedum (*Sedum rupestre*) doesn't like to stepped on, but it's a beauty for planting around the edge of a living patio.

# Lessons from the Living Patio

From a design perspective, a living patio provides a natural-looking transition between the house and the gardens around it. From a plant geek's point of view, it provides yet another place to experiment with cool ground covers and rock-garden plants. And for everyone, it creates a beautiful setting for outdoor entertaining, dining, or simply relaxing. Here are a couple of tips to help a living patio looking its best.

***Stock up on screenings before you start.*** Don't be tempted to rush the construction of your living patio, because it's far easier to do the job right at first than to try to fix uneven stones later. Once you get the orientation of each slab right, it's sometimes necessary to add some screenings (finely crushed rock, available at most quarries) under part of the rock to get it to sit level. Screenings are also a key ingredient in the mixture I use to "grout" between the stones: 1/3 loamy topsoil, 1/3 coarse sand, and 1/3 screenings (or small gravel). This blend provides good drainage but also holds some moisture, so it doesn't dry out too fast.

***Stop weeds before they start.*** It's a good idea to keep the spaces between the stones filled with paver plants, because weeds can easily sprout in uncovered soil. Plant all of the gaps thickly right at the start, and you'll reduce your

**Right plant for the right place.** Perennials that expand quickly by creeping roots, such as 'Fen's Ruby' cypress spurge (*Euphorbia cyparissias*) can be aggressive spreaders in the loose, rich soil of a bed or border, but they're perfect fillers for the tough conditions of a living patio.

weeding chores for the future. Apply-
ing pre-emergent weed control, such as
corn gluten meal, over any bare spots
that are visible in early spring will help to
prevent weed seeds from sprouting until
you can get around to filling the spaces
with transplants or new plants. If weeds
do sneak in over time, an old kitchen
knife or screwdriver is handy for prying
out the seedlings.

***Think ahead about winter.*** Keep in
mind that living patios can be tough to
shovel effectively after a snowfall without
damaging the plantings. If you plan one
for an area that you need access through

**Spread the wealth.** Don't depend on just one
kind of groundcover to fill the spaces in your living
patio. Using a variety of different plants adds much
more visual interest in every season. And if one
kind dies out for some reason, then the others can
spread to fill in the gaps that are left.

in winter, consider leaving your usual
path plant-free. Also, avoid using rock
salt on a living patio, because the so-
dium can build up in the soil and damage or kill the plants. Before winter,
pick up a bag of urea fertilizer at your
local garden center, so you have it on
hand if you really need to melt ice or
snow; it's far less likely than rock salt
to cause permanent plant damage.

# CHAPTER 6

# THE COTTAGE GARDEN

You know how it is with gardeners: where other people see a new fence or wall or path, we see an opportunity for creating a new garden. So it's hardly surprising that when we added the outbuilding we call the cottage in the winter of 2007, the cottage garden followed soon after.

## BEHIND THE DESIGN

People who know my penchant for finding interesting old outbuildings on my travels and hauling them back to Linden Hill often assume that the cottage is simply another of my acquisitions. This structure, though, was built entirely from scratch by master carpenter Ken Schuebel. It looks old because we built much of it with recycled materials. The 15- by 25-foot structure is framed with 200-year-old beams, for instance, while the flooring is composed of weathered oak planks, and the large sink is made from an old copper bathtub. The rustic interior creates the ideal ambience for our gift shop, where we carry Campo de' Fiori pottery and handcrafted artisan gifts. Such a building needed an equally charming exterior to welcome visitors to the space.

The layout of the garden around the cottage is fairly simple: the main part follows the outline of the building, extending out 10 to 12 feet from the foundation. An additional free-form island bed wraps around the southern side, separated from the main planting by a grass path that lets visitors walk through the garden as well as around it. Four large granite slabs form the steps up to the cottage door, with a cedar handrail for safety (and for planting on, as well).

## PICKING THE PLANTS

Even before the cottage was finished, my mind was full of ideas for all the combinations I wanted to try in the garden there. The actual planting, though, turned out to be a collaborative effort. You see, when my office manager, Cindi Sathra, and I were planning the Linden Hill plant events for the upcoming year, we both came up with the idea of having a "Cottage in the Country" theme for one weekend. And what could be more fun than giving our loyal customers the chance to make this garden their own with a hands-on planting workshop? It turned out that I was going to be in England at the very time we'd scheduled this event, so I added a few shrubs and trees first, then headed off on my travels.

**Starting with structure.** The cottage itself isn't all that tall, but it sits rather high on its site, so there really needed to be a few small trees and some shrubs to create a visual transition between the building and the flat lawn around it. 'Hearts of Gold' redbud (*Cercis canadensis*), with shocking pink flowers followed by chartreuse, heart-shaped leaves, got the most visible spot on the northeast corner, while another of my favorites, sweetbay magnolia (*Magnolia virginiana*), took the northwest corner. No cottage

39

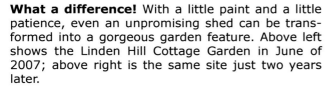

**What a difference!** With a little paint and a little patience, even an unpromising shed can be transformed into a gorgeous garden feature. Above left shows the Linden Hill Cottage Garden in June of 2007; above right is the same site just two years later.

garden would be complete without a fragrant mock orange (*Philadelphus coronarius*), so I added three of the golden-leaved 'Aureus' in this area as well. Around the back, I planted three Amur cherries (*Prunus maackii*) for their scented spring flowers as well as their beautiful golden brown bark, and a white-flowered 'Blanc Double de Coubert' rose (*Rosa rugosa*) too.

**Mixing it up.** Now it was our customers' turn. The day before the event, our staff had selected a wide variety of classic cottage-garden perennials and herbs and set them on the lawn next to the cottage. The collection included a number of catmints (*Nepeta*), dianthus, hardy geraniums, irises, phlox, and salvias, as well as bee balms (*Monarda*), bellflowers (*Campanula*), columbines (*Aquilegia*), lady's mantle (*Alchemilla mollis*), lamb's ears (*Stachys byzantina*), lupines (*Lupinus*), peonies, purple coneflowers (*Echinacea*), thymes (*Thymus*), veronicas, yarrows (*Achillea*), and many other flowering favorites. After giving a brief introduction to the cottage-garden planting style, our staff turned the workshop participants loose to select the plants they liked best and worked side-by-side with them to get the garden planted.

Watching the garden develop as the plants filled out through their first season was an adventure for all of us. Some people teased me about getting a garden planted with "free labor," but our customers considered it great fun, and many of them come back regularly to admire the garden and see how the plants they chose are performing.

## OVER THE YEARS

Since that first season, we've expanded on the cottage-garden theme further by adding many more herbs for flavor and fragrance, including basils, curry plant (*Helichrysum angustifolium*), golden lemon balm (*Melissa officinalis* 'All Gold), and culinary sages (*Salvia officinalis*). And what would a traditional cottage garden be without vegetables? Each year, we tuck in different veggies that are attractive as well as edible, among them multi-colored 'Bright Lights' chard, purple 'Kolibri' kohlrabi, blue 'Lacinato' kale, spiky-leaved onions, and silvery 'Violetta' artichokes.

**An incredible edible.** If you're looking for veggies that do double-duty as ornamentals, it's tough to beat 'Ruby Perfection' cabbage for beautiful foliage color and dramatic form.

Heirloom annuals, set out as transplants or sown directly into any empty spots, make great cottage-garden fillers and provide extra spots of seasonal color. Some of our favorites include forget-me-nots (*Myosotis*), larkspurs (*Consolida*), love-in-a-mist (*Nigella damascena*), nasturtiums (*Tropaeolum majus*), various poppies (*Papaver*), and violas.

So far, the biggest change we've made to the original planting was in the fall of 2008, when we took out a sickly-looking lilac and added a good-sized 'Butterflies' magnolia at the southeast corner of the cottage. My original intent

in adding it was to create a sense of enclosure to the space between the cottage and our office, and to provide some summer shade as well. Soon after it was in place, though, the beautiful gray bark and big fuzzy buds that were evident once the leaves dropped inspired yet another idea: a small winter garden.

Staff member Tom Dermody replaced part of what had been a grass path with large stepping stones, prepared a new planting bed between the path and the office, and set about filling both the new bed and the space around and under the magnolia with a variety of plants for cool-season color, including a 'Hedgerows Gold' dogwood (*Cornus sericea*) for its bright red bark, many heucheras for purple, orange, peach and coppery foliage, hellebores (*Helleborus*) for evergreen foliage and early bloom, and many kinds of minor bulbs. We have no doubt, though, that the true stars of the show will be the yellow spring flowers of that magnolia!

**Growing up.** Always on the lookout for ways to squeeze in more plants, we couldn't resist planting the hand rail for the cottage steps too. Last year, it supported a 'Heavenly Blue' morning glory (*Ipomoea*) as well as a 'Sungold' cherry tomato, which held its flavorful orange fruits at a perfect height for picking as we passed by.

# Lessons from the Cottage Garden

Quaint and quirky, fun and whimsical – cottage gardens are all that and more. We're continually making changes in the Linden Hill Cottage Garden: adding vines and climbers to dress up the walls, shifting plants around, and nestling in bird houses and other rustic ornaments for display as well as decoration. It's hard to take a casual space like this too seriously – and that makes it a true joy to putter around in.

***Anything goes.*** There's pretty much no design in a cottage garden, so you simply can't do it wrong. Forget about the "rule" of planting in groups of 3 or 5 or 7; if you have or want only one of something, that's fine. This relaxed style makes a cottage garden a perfect setting for experimenting with new plants. The relaxed atmosphere also makes it a super place to get kids

involved in gardening and excited about flowers, herbs, and veggies. My daughter Lily had great fun selecting perennials and choosing what she felt were the perfect places for them when we planted the winter corner – and we had great fun watching her.

***Welcome volunteers.*** Self-sowing annuals and perennials, such as black-eyed Susans (*Rudbeckia*), flowering tobaccos (*Nicotiana*), forget-me-nots (*Myosotis*), love-in-a-mist (*Nigella damascena*), and lady's mantle (*Alchemilla mollis*), are key ingredients in any cottage garden. You never know where they're going to pop up next year – perhaps in a path, or nestled up next to a taller companion – but they have a knack for creating beautiful pairings that you'd never have thought of on your own. Plus, they're great at filling spaces that might otherwise have been empty, which saves a lot of weeding time through the season.

**The supporting cast.** When one of the Amur cherries (*Prunus maackii*) that we planted started to die, we didn't have a replacement handy, so we left it in place for the rest of the season and used it as a support for a cardinal climber (*Ipomoea* x *multifida*) vine and a cherry tomato, too.

**Out-of-the-ordinary annuals.** Cottage gardens are great places to try out new plants. A few of our experiments from previous years include 'Cramer's Plum' love-in-a-mist (*Nigella damascena*), above left; widow's tears (*Tinantia erecta*), top right; and variegated kiss-me-over-the-garden-gate (*Persicaria orientalis* 'Variegata'), at right.

***Making the most of rainwater.*** I decided against putting a gutter on the back roof of the Linden Hill cottage, so the rain water could run off directly into the garden and be absorbed by the soil. There did need to be one in front, though, to keep it from dripping onto the doorstep. But instead of adding a downspout, which would have directed all of the runoff water into one spot and possibly caused erosion, I hung a copper rain chain. Visitors often admire its decorative qualities, but it serves a practical function as well, slowing down the flow of the water and giving it a chance to soak into the soil, which in turn cuts down on our watering time between rains.

# CHAPTER 7

# THE DEER-RESISTANT GARDEN

When I started my landscape design business 20 years ago, I'd usually start the interview with a new client by asking about their favorite colors, or if they wanted fragrance in the garden. Now, the first question is always "Do you have deer?" This is by far the most important factor for anyone planning a garden in the Delaware Valley, as well as in many other areas. Our customers know it, too! We set up a special table in our sales area to showcase deer-resistant plants, so when deer-plagued gardeners come in to shop, we can show them an assortment of perennials and shrubs that they're likely to succeed with.

We eventually came up with the idea of going one step further and creating an entire garden. based on deer-resistant plants. It came to reality when my dear friend Dan Heims of Terra Nova Nurseries was visiting and suggested that I ask Nancy Ondra to co-design it with me. Within hours, she and I were discussing the project, and within two months, the garden was getting started.

## BEHIND THE DESIGN

It would have been easier for our customers if we had located the planting closer to our sales area, but we wanted a true test, so we chose a site a bit further away that included an active deer trail near our pond. To add to the challenge, we decided to develop this wide-open area into a woodland-like setting, which seems to be the favored habitat of deer and is where their browsing habits can be particularly devastating. A final key feature of the project was to be an evergreen planting along the property line to screen a neighboring business and give the garden a handsome backdrop.

Phase One of the garden, in the fall of 2007, involved removing the existing turf with a sod cutter, preparing the soil, adding a gently winding, 6-foot-wide, gravel path through the center of the area (which ended up being about 200 feet long and 65 feet wide), and installing the trees, the shrubs, and some perennials.

Phase Two of the Deer-Resistant Garden began in spring of 2008, with the addition of more herbaceous plants, and continued into early summer. Along with planting many dozens more perennials, Nancy, Jessica Myers, Marcos Gomez, and many other staff members tucked in many hundreds of potted flowering and foliage annuals to fill space around the still-young perennials.

Besides displaying an extensive variety of deer-resistant options, this planting does double-duty as a color-theme garden. The western end features mostly silvers, whites, and blues, transitioning to blue, light yellow, pink, and peachy flowers with chartreuse and purple foliage toward the middle and finally to vibrant reds, oranges, purples, and yellows at the eastern end.

## PICKING THE PLANTS

A simple web search can bring up thousands of lists of deer-resistant plants. Unfortunately, deer

EARLY
SPRING
2008

EARLY
FALL
2008

don't read those lists. Like people, they have different tastes, and those preferences vary from region to region. And if they get hungry enough, they'll nibble on or even devour plants that they normally wouldn't touch. Generally speaking, deer don't like plants that are spiny, fuzzy, or aromatic. But at a client's property, I once saw an entire planting of pungently scented culinary sage (*Salvia officinalis*) that had been reduced to mere stubs from deer damage.

Still, we had to start somewhere, so the Linden Hill Deer-Resistant Garden is based on plants that have normally not been bothered by deer in our part of Bucks County. We then filled in with those that have traditionally been considered deer-resistant, as well as some lesser-known plants that we wanted to test.

**Starting with structure.** The first addition to the space was a grove of five good-sized American hornbeams (*Carpinus caroliniana*) to provide shade and screening from the open side of the garden. On the other side of the path, we created evergreen screening with a row of 'Green Giant' arborvitae (*Thuja plicata*), a fast-grower that can often put on 3 feet of new growth per year. We set the plants at close spacings for quick cover, knowing that we could thin them out later if needed. (I should note here that arborvitae typically *aren't* deer-resistant, but it's what we had on hand in our holding beds, and I thought it would be worth the gamble that the deer-resistant plantings in front of them would prevent them from being damaged. So far, so good!) Other trees we added for height and shade included red oak and willow oak (*Quercus rubra* and *Q. phellos*), sweet gum (*Liquidambar styraciflua*), and a witch hazel (*Hamamelis virginiana*).

A variety of shrubs make up the understory in the Deer-Resistant Garden. Among the deciduous shrubs are 'Anabelle' smooth hydrangea (*Hydrangea arborescens*), bottlebrush buckeye (*Aesculus parviflora*), butterfly bushes (*Buddleia*), buttonbush (*Cephalanthus occidentalis*), 'Flying Dragon' hardy

**Foliage features.** This silvery trio of 'Grosso' lavender (*Lavandula* x *intermedia*), 'Big Ears' lambs ears (*Stachys byzantina*), and 'Powis Castle' artemisia features fuzzy and aromatic foliage, both of which may be less attractive to deer.

orange (*Poncirus trifoliata*), fothergillas (*Fothergilla*), fragrant abelia (*Abelia mosanensis*), golden mockorange (*Philadelphus coronarius* 'Aureus'), hypericums (*Hypericum*), 'Kumson' forsythia (*Forsythia viridissima*), nandinas (*Nandina*), smoke bush (*Cotinus coggygria*), spireas (*Spiraea*), sweetfern (*Comptonia peregrina*), and sweetspire (*Itea virginica*). Additions for evergreen interest include various boxwoods (*Buxus*), 'Duke's Gardens' plum yew (*Cephalotaxus harringtonii*), dwarf pieris (*Pieris japonica* 'Pygmaea'), 'Goshiki' false holly (*Osmanthus heterophyllus*), 'Picturata' Japanese aucuba (*Aucuba japonica*), and sweet box (*Sarcococca hookeriana* var. *humilis*).

**Mixing it up.** Even staying away from known "deer candy," such as hostas and daylilies

**Elegant intensity.** Gardens that are deer-resistant can be beautiful too. The hot-color section of our planting features combinations of richly hued foliage and flowers, such as vibrant blue 'May Night' sage (*Salvia*), yellow 'Baggesen's Gold' boxleaf honeysuckle (*Lonicera nitida*), orange cosmos, purple-leaved coleus and basil, and red-flowered 'Lucifer' crocosmia.

(*Hemerocallis*), we still had an abundance of herbaceous plants to try. There are many fuzzy-leaved options, for instance, including avens (*Geum*), 'Big Ears' lamb's ears (*Stachys byzantina*), forget-me-nots (*Myosotis*), hairy bergenia (*Bergenia ciliata*), 'Hidcote Blue' comfrey (*Symphytum*), Jerusalem sage (*Phlomis russeliana*), lungworts (*Pulmonaria*), and Siberian bugloss (*Brunnera macrophylla*).

Deer usually don't like aromatic foliage, but gardeners do, so we included plenty of that too, including bee balms (*Monarda*), bigroot geranium (*Geranium macrorrhizum*), catmints (*Nepeta*), golden feverfew (*Tanacetum parthenium* 'Aureum'), golden lemon balm (*Melissa officinalis* 'All Gold'), golden oregano (*Origanum vulgare* 'Aureum'), perennial sages (*Salvia*), 'Powis Castle' artemisias, thymes (*Thymus*), 'White Cloud' calamint (*Calamintha*), and yarrows (*Achillea*).

Then there are the time-tested favorites that have proven to be less palatable to deer in our area, among them common bleeding heart (*Dicentra spectabilis*), epimediums, euphorbias, globeflowers (*Trollius*), hellebores (*Helleborus*), Jacob's ladders (*Polemonium*), meadow rues (*Thalictrum*), meadowsweet (*Filipendula ul-*

*maria* 'Aurea' and 'Variegata'), 'Sheffield Pink' chrysanthemum, Solomon's seals (*Polygonatum*), and variegated Japanese iris (*Iris kaempferi* 'Variegata'). Many ornamental grasses, too, proved to be trouble-free, including various fountain grasses (*Pennisetum*), purple moor grasses (*Molinia caerulea*), sedges (*Carex*), and switch grasses (*Panicum virgatum*). Ferns, as well, were a must-try for the shadier spots, so we added cinnamon fern (*Osmunda cinnamomea*), Japanese painted fern (*Athyrium niponicum* var. *pictum*), and lady fern (*Athyrium filix-femina*).

For the first summer, especially, we wanted to add lots of annuals to fill the spaces around the newly planted perennials: partly to cut down on weeding and partly to make a big splash of color. We also noticed that annuals are often left out of lists of deer-resistant plants, so we thought this would be a great opportunity to trial some. Among those that thrived and created a stunning show included amaranths (*Amaranthus*), angelonias, bloodflower (*Asclepias curassavica*), browallia (*Browallia americana*), coleus, lantanas, periwinkle (*Catharanthus roseus*), polka-dot plants (*Hypoestes phyllostachys*), portulacas, annual and tender sages (*Salvia*), snow on the mountain (*Euphorbia marginata*), variegated kiss-me-over-the-garden-gate (*Persicaria orientalis* 'Shiro-gane Nishiki'), verbenas, and many kinds of zinnias.

## OVER THE YEARS

By the end of its first year, the Deer-Resistant Garden was deemed to be a rousing success on many levels. Though we did see signs of deer in that area — hoofprints here and there, and the occasional annual or perennial knocked down — they didn't cause any feeding damage. Our customers and clients loved having the opportunity to see for themselves that they really *could* have a beautiful garden even in deer country.

Now, I have to be honest and say that while the garden did prove to be deer-resistant, it unfortunately wasn't resistant to *all* pests. During the first summer, a series of groundhogs moved in and were particularly persistent about feeding on

the sweet potato vines (*Ipomoea batatas*). We also had some troubles with voles and mice tunneling under the dense herbaceous layer, so we pulled out the annuals and cut back all of the perennials in October to remove their hiding places, which seemed to stop the damage from progressing.

Removing the annuals that early left plenty of empty space, and the weather was still perfect for planting, so we took the opportunity do some tweaking: removing plants that had turned out to be mislabeled and dividing vigorous perennials that had outgrown their allotted space. Then we added hundreds more perennials throughout the planting, including a variety of ephemeral wildflowers and native groundcovers to fill the shady spots under the trees and shrubs.

With those additions of perennials and self-sown seedlings from the annuals, we anticipate that this garden won't need much more additional planting from this point, except for gradual replacement of the sun-lovers with more shade-tolerant plants as the woody plants fill in and cast more shade. And, of course, we'll continue to trial new plants that our customers and clients tell us have proven to be problem-free for them, so we can continue to spread the word about the delights of deer-resistant gardening in southeastern Pennsylvania.

**Stunning in silver.** This cool combination of bold cardoon (*Cynara cardunculus*), 'Cora White' rose periwinkle (*Catharanthus roseus*), and brushy 'Little Bunny' fountain grass (*Pennisetum alopecurioides*) marks the entrance to the Linden Hill Deer-Resistant Garden.

49

# Lessons from the Deer-Resistant Garden

There's nothing like seeing the delight on the faces of deer-plagued gardeners when they realize that there really *is* hope: that there really *are* plants those four-footed menaces seem to find less palatable than others. What works for us at Linden Hill may not be equally successful in other areas, though, so you'll want to grab every chance you can to find out what other gardeners in your own neighborhood have luck with. Garden tours are an great opportunity to see local plantings for yourself, and to ask the gardeners who care for them about their particular disappointments and successes.

***More deer deterrents.*** Repellent sprays add an extra level of protection to deer-resistant plantings. One that we've had luck with at Linden Hill is plain old fish emulsion diluted according to the label directions and applied with a hose-end sprayer. Besides discouraging deer, it supplies nutrients to the plants. As with the plants themselves, you'll probably need to experiment with different kinds to find out what works best for your particular garden. Keep in mind, too, that you may need to rotate using two or three different kinds so your local deer don't get used to them.

**Get the point?** Only the most desperate deer would even think about snacking on this stunning spiny wonder: an annual or tender perennial commonly known as bed-of-nails or naranjilla (*Solanum quitoense*).

**Better together.** We created our woodland setting from scratch by setting out rather large trees, but you could easily make your own by linking several existing trees and shrubs into one or more larger beds. Along with giving you all kinds of exciting planting opportunities, this will save you loads of time mowing, trimming, and mulching around individual trees and shrubs.

**Discouraging other diners.** People often ask us if deer-resistant plants are also resistant to damage from other animals. Spiny or strongly aromatic plants sometimes deter rabbits too, but generally, the answer is no. In our own garden, we occasionally have problems with groundhog damage, and with voles tunneling through the crowns of our perennials, as shown above left. We've started planting bulbs of various *Fritillaria* species, such as crown imperials (*F. imperialis*), above right, throughout the gardens, hoping that their strong musky scent will protect their companions from both deer and voles, at least.

**Divide and conquer.** Starting a new garden can be daunting when you have estate-garden dreams on a home-garden budget. But you can save yourself hundreds or even thousands of dollars on plants with one simple trick: building and using holding beds. Set up one or more planting areas in an out-of-the-way spot in your yard, then fill them with home-grown seedlings, acquisitions from plant swaps, gifts from other gardeners, and bargains from garden-center sales. Leave them in place for a season or two, then divide the perennials when they are large enough and replant them in the holding beds to bulk up again. In just a few years, you can have plenty of plants to fill even a large garden all at once without spending a fortune.

# CHAPTER 8

# MOUNT LINDEN

When I was little, I spent many happy hours in an empty spot in my family's vegetable garden with my Tonka truck and toy excavator, building up a pile of soil and then sculpting roads into the sides of it. In that, I wasn't so different from many other young boys. But unlike many others, I've had the chance to make my childhood visions come true, and Linden Hill's mount — which we jokingly refer to as Mount Linden — is part of that adventure.

## BEHIND THE DESIGN

It wasn't exactly a straight line from my original small pile of soil to the quite large one we have now. In fact, I'd forgotten about the idea for quite a while, and it wasn't in my plans as I began to develop the Linden Hill property. In the spring of 2008, I was working on fulfilling another dream — of getting some farm animals — and we were laying out a pasture for the four lambs that were coming to live at Linden Hill. I was contemplating the area of flat land left next to the pasture and suddenly remembered the trip I'd taken to England the previous year, when I'd visited Sissinghurst and climbed to the top of the brick tower, which overlooks the gardens. Wouldn't it be neat to have a lookout point like that here?

Creating a structure like Sissinghurst's brick tower wasn't in the budget, so I thought about what else I might be able to use. One day,

I realized that I already had a great resource on hand: a huge pile of compost and topsoil that had accumulated from five years' worth of garden-making and maintenance from both Linden Hill and our clients' properties. I could use that to make a giant-sized version of the soil piles I had loved as a kid! I called local excavator Ed Litzenberger to tell him my idea, and 10 minutes later, Ed and I were walking the site and discussing the project. The next day, three of his workers arrived with earth-moving equipment and shifted approximately 3000 cubic yards of the compost/soil blend to create a pile about 20 feet high and 60 feet wide. We let it sit for a week, finished the basic grading to smooth out the conical shape, and then thought about planting it.

## PICKING THE PLANTS

I wanted to let the whole mount settle for at least a year before cutting in the paths and doing the final planting. But it still needed some kind of groundcover to stabilize the soil and prevent erosion, so I decided to sow it with annual ryegrass for the first season. The sod kept the soil in place, then died off over the winter.

Historically, mounts have been planted either with trees and shrubs or with turf. I thought it would be interesting to create a meadow-like effect with native grasses accented with a sprinkling of flowers. In the future, I plan to cut a spiral path

THE
BEGINNING

THE
BUILDING

THE
GRADING

THE
GROWING

around the mound to create an easy ascent to the top. Then we'll replace the annual ryegrass with little bluestem (*Schizachyrium scoparium*) and other native grasses, and dot Brazilian vervain (*Verbena bonariensis*) throughout to give some extra height and color. Eventually, we'll add daffodils and other bulbs for spring interest, too.

## OVER THE YEARS

Needless to say, Mount Linden has caused quite a stir among our customers. It's not a feature you often see in American gardens, after all, especially in the North. (There are still a few old garden mounts in the southern United States, but they were never all that common here, being more commonly associated with English landscapes from the 16th through the 18th centuries.) Visitors of all ages enjoy climbing up to the top to enjoy an aerial view of the gardens and nursery, and we've had landscape clients express interest in having a mount created on their own property.

A mount is such a prominent feature that it can be difficult to integrate into the rest of landscape. But really, the prominence is the very *point* of a mount, so instead of trying to get the Linden Hill mount to blend in, I decided to accentuate it further with another distinctive feature: a double row of granite slabs set on end to create an allee of standing stones leading directly from the sales area to the base of the mount. This seems to draw visitors out into the landscape instead of just looking at it from a distance. And once they're out there, few can resist climbing up for a better view.

**The finished product.** Mount Linden in late July of 2008, with an allee of granite posts leading up to it.

# Lessons from Mount Linden

Granted, most homeowners don't have the space to create a mount as big as Mount Linden in their backyard. But even a much more modest raised area can be a welcome addition to an otherwise flat property, giving you a whole different perspective of the space. You might be able to create a mini-mount with soil excavated for a pool or some other landscape project.

**Shaping it up.** A mount can be any shape you want: conical, domed, rectangular, or even free-form. Just keep in mind that if the sides are very steep or irregular, mowing even just once a year can be a big challenge, and you may have erosion problems, too. Whatever shape you choose, I highly recommend creating a flat space on top for a bench or seat. Once you get up there, it's tempting to hang out for a while to enjoy the view.

**The thrill of a hill.** I can practically guarantee you that a mount of any size will quickly become the favorite play area of any kids in the family. A small mount can still provide ample scope for the imagination; a large one can provide endless fun for winter sledding or snowboarding.

**Consider a meadow mound.** If you have an on-lot septic disposal system commonly called a "sand mound," you already have a mount without even realizing it! Sand mounds are typically planted with turf grass and kept mowed as turf, but (if local regulations permit) you could instead cover yours with a mix of low-growing native grasses and wildflowers, such as little bluestem (*Schizachyrium scoparium*), prairie dropseed (*Sporobolus heterolepis*), butterfly weed (*Asclepias tuberosa*), and coneflowers (*Echinacea* and *Rudbeckia*). A meadow mound needs mowing only once a year, reducing the maintenance chores, minimizing compaction to the mound, and turning an eyesore into a beautiful addition to the landscape.

**Country casual.** A mount can be a great place for a meadow planting, providing beauty and wildlife habitat as it changes through the season and over the years. Below is a sand mound meadow in midsummer of its third year; above is the same planting in early fall, two years later.

**Slip sliding away (opposite page).** For a summer party here at Linden Hill, we set up a temporary water slide on Mount Linden with hay bales and a sheet of plastic. It kept the kids (and some adults, too) entertained for hours.

# PART TWO
## IDEAS AND INSPIRATION

# CHAPTER 9

# JERRY'S TOP-10 PLANTS

Asking gardeners to choose a few favorite plants is almost like asking them to choose a favorite child. It's easy to love them all! But when I think about the plants that I tend to use frequently, here at Linden Hill and in my own and clients' gardens, I realize that I depend heavily on a small number of workhorse perennials, shrubs, and trees. Some have outstanding flowers, some have exceptional foliage, and several have both. Most importantly, they all have been top performers here in the mid-Atlantic region. I've tried to limit myself to just 10. We'll see if I succeed. I've put the perennials first, followed by the woody plants; beyond that, they're in no particular order.

## EXQUISITE IRISES

I could easily fill my list with nothing but irises if I treated them individually, so I'll count the whole group of them as one pick. There's something so regal about the look of these classic perennials, and they come in an amazing array of heights and colors, with species and hybrids to suit just about any growing conditions. Here are a few of my particular favorites.

**'Immortality'.** I consider the hybrid bearded iris 'Immortality' the best of the best. Its pristine white blooms don't appear just once in midsummer, as those of most beardeds do; it dependably flowers again in late summer to early fall, and sometimes even a third time later in fall. Add in its pleasant fragrance and good-

looking, gray-green foliage, and you get one high-performance perennial.

**Siberian iris (*Iris sibirica*).** Of all the flower colors to choose from, the range I'm most often drawn to is the blue-purples — the "blurples," as I like to call them — and few other

**Bearded iris 'Immortality' with 'Twilite Prairieblues' false indigo (*Baptisia*)**

plants offer so many tints and shades of these hues. You can also find cultivars and hybrids that bloom in white and yellow, which are elegant on their own and outstanding mingled with the blues and purples. Siberian irises can tolerate the heavy clay soil that's the kiss of death for more delicate perennials, and they even adapt well to soggy sites. They're both beautiful and tough – what more can you ask for?

**Variegated Japanese iris (Iris ensata 'Variegata').** The large, velvety violet-purple flowers of Japanese iris grace the garden in mid- to late June, on quick-growing plants that perform just fine in average garden soil: all good enough reasons to grow it. But this selection offers yet another great feature: bold white striping on its normally plain green, sword-like leaves. This dramatic variegation turns the single-season species into an exceptional perennial for spring-through-fall interest. I particularly like planting it in front of evergreens with deep green leaves, such as hollies (*Ilex*) or boxwoods (*Buxus*), because the dark background really makes the iris foliage "pop."

**Variegated Japanese iris (*Iris ensata* 'Variegata') with *Sedum* 'Black Jack'**

## LOVELY LENTEN ROSES

Lenten roses (*Helleborus* x *hybridus*) don't get nearly as much attention as irises, maybe because hellebores bloom well before that peak May-June period when most people pay attention to gardens. And when they *do* flower, they don't have the in-your-face color of crocuses, daffodils and many other bulbs that adorn the garden at the same time. I don't consider either of these factors as reasons to overlook Lenten roses, though. I'm a big fan of the traditional English-style border that's spectacular in late spring and early summer, but that's just two months out of the whole year. After our long, cold Pennsylvania winters, I'm ready to get out into the garden in February or March, and I can always count on Lenten roses to spring into bloom as soon as the ground starts to thaw.

Though Lenten roses lack the visible-from-100-yards away showiness of some early bloomers, their more delicate beauty makes it worth taking a few extra minutes to walk over and admire them. What a great excuse to take a stroll outside on those first days when spring seems possible again! Many breeders are working on selecting fancier flower forms, and on developing Lenten roses that hold their flowers upward. But I still like the simple elegance of the lightly cupped singles, and I enjoy touching the nodding blooms to tip their faces up and appreciate them at close range. I also like to plant them on a hillside or along the top of a retaining wall, where I can look up into the flowers.

Their show is generally finished around the end of April, but by then, a flush of new foliage is coming up from the ground. The leaves start off bright green, darkening to a rich deep green, and they stick around through the winter, providing welcome winter interest.

On top of all that, deer *usually* leave Lenten roses alone. Yes, despite the many claims to the contrary, hellebores are not totally deer-proof. But the plants apparently aren't very tasty, so deer tend to pass them by if they can find anything else to eat. No surprise, then, that we plant a *lot* of Lenten roses here at Linden Hill!

**Lenten rose (*Helleborus* x *hybridus*)**

63

## MAGICAL MYOSOTIS

The whites, yellows, pinks, purples, and reds of Lenten roses are all welcome colors in the early garden, but they have one lack: no true blues. After months of looking at white snow and brown soil, I'm positively craving a shot of my most favorite color, so I turn to another sure sign of the coming spring: the cheery blue blooms of forget-me-nots (*Myosotis*). Some gardeners treat these plants as annuals, planting them in early spring and then pulling them out as soon as the flowers finish. I prefer to let them go to seed and then cut them back to about 1 inch above the ground. Sometimes

**'Ultramarine' forget-me-not (*Myosotis*) with Bowles' golden sedge (*Carex elata* 'Aurea') and *Heuchera* 'Caramel'**

I make a point of shaking the seed-laden tops over other parts of the garden to ensure new plants for next spring, but the seeds seem to spread out on their own even without my help, and the original plants often resprout as well, acting more like perennials than annuals or biennials.

Forget-me-nots create carpets of early color that brighten spaces under still-bare deciduous trees and shrubs, finishing up around the time that their taller partners leaf out and shade the ground. Like Lenten roses, forget-me-nots are also deer-resistant. In fact, these two groups of plants are so compatible in terms of heights, bloom times, and preferred growing conditions that I can't think of a better pairing for spring color in a spot that turns shady by summer.

## GRACEFUL FOREST GRASS

I call it variegated Japanese forest grass; you may know it as golden Hakone grass. By any name, *Hakonechloa macra* 'Aureola' is a beauty: hands-down my favorite ornamental grass for shady to partly sunny sites. It contributes eye-catching color from the time it sprouts in mid-spring through a few frosts in fall, with arching, lemon yellow leaves that are thinly striped with green, creating a solid-chartreuse effect from any distance. The return of cold weather brings out reddish to pinkish streaking in the foliage, which eventually ages to golden brown as it dies off in winter.

Japanese forest grass grows in well-behaved, slowly expanding clumps; no worries about it creeping around and crowding out other plants. In fact, I wish it would fill out a little faster, because I can't get enough of it! Its cascading mounds of foliage are perfect for softening the edges of borders and walkways, and they're fantastic in containers, too. The bright

**Variegated Japanese wind grass (*Hakonechloa macra 'Aureola'*)**

variegated Japanese wind grass I mentioned above is one good example: its dainty golden bronze flowerheads are nice but hardly showy compared to the leaves. Another of my top picks for terrific foliage color and texture is 'Angelina' sedum (*Sedum rupestre*). You may not even notice when 'Angelina' blooms, in fact, because the yellow flowers pretty much blend in with the plant's bright yellow spring-to-fall foliage.

foliage looks especially good in contrast with dark-leaved partners, such as hostas, ferns, and Lenten roses, and it's not much bothered by deer. I'm excited to see other selections of Japanese wind grass coming on the market, such as the solid-chartreuse 'All Gold', green-and-white-striped 'Albovariegata', and green-tipped-with-red 'Beni-kaze'. The original 'Aureola' is still my favorite, though.

## A MUST-SEE SEDUM

It's easy to focus on flowers when selecting perennials, but I encourage you to give the foliage a good look too. The leaves are around all season, after all, while the flowers come and go. If you find a plant that you'd find appealing even if it never flowered, you've discovered a winner for multi-season interest in your garden. That

It would be enough to have even that much dependable foliage interest, but 'Angelina' takes it one step further by being evergreen – or maybe I should say "ever-yellow." No, even that doesn't really give you the full picture. When cold weather returns in autumn, the tip of each shoot begins to blush, turning from dull rust to a vibrant orange-red and holding that color through the winter months. Walking along a path edged with 'Angelina' is guaranteed to brighten your day, no matter what the weather or season.

'Angelina' is no prima donna perennial, either: once she's in the ground, she'll spread out readily and make herself right at home with little fussing from the gardener. In fact, if you leave the flowers on, she'll self-sow readily. She especially likes to seed into gravel paths, but her babies will also come up among other perennials, sometimes

**'Angelina' sedum (*Sedum rupestre*) in winter**

creating great combination completely by chance. The seedlings have the same bright yellow leaves as 'Angelina', so it's easy enough to spot them and pull or dig them out if you don't want them. Chances are you have a use for all the seedlings you find, though, as fillers at the front of a border, on slopes, or in living patios. They look super tucked into containers, too: planters, window boxes, and even hanging baskets.

## NOW, FOR NEPETAS

Well, what can I say? I've been known to design catmints (*Nepeta*) into gardens now and again. In fact, they're one of my signature plants: my go-to perennials for pretty much any sunny garden. And why not? I like them for their aromatic (and deer-resistant!) gray-green foliage, but what I really love them for is their flower color: the "blurples" that I simply can't get enough of. Their soft blue-purple hues are very calming, giving gardens a more relaxed appearance, and their delicate haziness has a way of making even small spaces look larger.

There are a number of species, hybrids, and cultivars to choose from: 'Walker's Low' and 'Joanna Reed' are two of my favorites. Both of these are supposed to be sterile, which means that they put their energy into a long bloom period instead of producing seed; it also minimizes or eliminates getting unwanted seedlings. Flowering tends to start early — usually in May — and continues while the plants expand into low mounds. By late July or early August, most catmints can get a little floppy, and their first flush of bloom is about over. At that point, I like to chop them back to about 2 inches, which encourages the plants to produce fresh mounds of good-looking foliage and more flowers well into fall. That's a total of about 5 months of bloom: a great performance from one adaptable, easy-care perennial!

## HEAVENLY HYDRANGEAS

And now, I have to add some of my favorite woody plants. I feel the same way about hydrangeas as I do about irises – I simply can't get enough of them – so I'm going to count the bunch of them as one pick. These classic garden beauties have an old-fashioned charm but can look equally good in more modern settings, and there's a wide range of heights, habits, and colors to choose from for both sun and shade. Here are three of the kinds I use most.

**Bigleaf hydrangea (*Hydrangea macrophylla*).** I adore bigleaf hydrangeas: the older summer-blooming cultivars like 'Ayesha', with distinctively cupped pink-to-blue petals, and 'Domotoi', with large, double flowers, as well as the newer repeat-bloomers, such as the Endless Summer and Forever & Ever selections. This is the group that can vary in color according to the soil pH: acidic conditions favor good blues, while alkaline soil generally develops good pinks.

**Panicle hydrangea (*H. paniculata*).** These white-flowered summer wonders are eye-catching during the day and positively glow in the evening garden. By fall, the flowers have mostly blushed to a pinkish cream color that looks terrific

**Walker's Low' catmint (*Nepeta*) with lady's mantle (*Alchemilla mollis*)**

**'Unique' hydrangea (*Hydrangea paniculata*) with 'Walker's Low' catmint (*Nepeta*)**

in cut-flower arrangements. Unlike bigleaf hydrangea, which tends to bloom on shoots that formed the previous year, panicle hydrangeas flower on the current year's shoots. For that reason, I recommend pruning all panicle hydrangeas every year in late winter, cutting them down to about 3 feet above the ground, to get an abundance of free-flowering new growth.

**Climbing hydrangea (*H. anomala* subsp. *petiolaris*).** Most hydrangeas grow as shrubs, but this one grows as a stately, woody-stemmed climber. Trained on a wall, it creates an espalier-like effect; attached to a tall post, it's a dramatic vertical accent. Or, let it trail horizontally to create a handsome groundcover; it looks especially good on a slope, and it's great for covering up old stumps, too. The lacy flower clusters of climbing hydrangea appear in June and show off beautifully against the deep green summer foliage. In fall, the leaves turn an attractive golden color, then drop to reveal the attractively peeling stems for winter interest. It's truly a four-season plant!

## A PEERLESS SPIREA

You may see this top-notch deciduous shrub sold under its cultivar name 'Ogon' or its trademarked name Mellow Yellow. It's a winner either way, for its wonderful chartreuse foliage as well as its fragrant flowers, fantastic fall color, and natural billowing form. Unlike many of the other yellow-leaved spireas, which tend to produce pink flowers

**Climbing hydrangea (*Hydrangea anomala* subsp. *petiolaris*)**

**Mellow Yellow spirea (*Spiraea thunbergii* 'Ogon') in bloom**

with their foliage in summer, this selection of *Spiraea thunbergii* blooms far earlier: usually in March for us. The slender, leafless stems are lined with countless tiny, white flowers just in time to pair perfectly with violas and early spring bulbs, such as grape hyacinths (*Muscari*). New foliage starts to appear about the time the flowers are finished.

Left alone, 'Ogon' can eventually reach 4 to 5 feet tall and wide, but you can easily keep it smaller by pruning it back hard — even as low as about 1 foot above the ground — in spring. (I

**Mellow Yellow spirea (*Spiraea thunbergii* 'Ogon') with bearded iris 'Immortality'**

usually like to wait until the flowers are finished, but you could shear it earlier if you want.) While the plants can tolerate some shade, full sun brings out the best summer foliage color, and it also encourages the richest orangey red hues to develop before the leaves drop in late fall. Did I mention that 'Ogon' is deer-resistant too? If you don't already have an 'Ogon' in your garden, go get one right now. You'll thank me later!

## THE SWEETEST MAGNOLIA

Small trees are so handy from a design standpoint. In large landscapes, they help to create an important visual transition between the lower perennials and shrubs and the taller-growing shade trees. And in smaller gardens, they add much-needed height while staying in proportion to the space. There are quite a few to choose from, but I think my top pick here has to be sweetbay magnolia (*Magnolia virginiana*).

This charming native has an open, airy branching habit that lets plenty of light through to the ground, so I like to underplant it with spring wildflowers, small bulbs, and early perennials. It leafs out in a lovely soft shade of medium green that complements the riot of color that's going closer to ground level in late spring. Then in June, it starts opening its own creamy white blooms, which release an intoxicating spicy-vanilla scent.

The bloom display is mostly over in July, but occasional new blooms appear through the rest of the summer. From late summer into fall, the flowers mature into greenish fruits which darken and split open when they're mature, revealing bright orange-red seeds to delight the gardener — and some fruit-eating birds, too.

**Sweetbay magnolia (*Magnolia virginiana*)**

Evergreen in warmer climates, sweetbay magnolia normally loses its leaves for the winter here in Pennsylvania. There are still the light green stems of the newer shoots for some color interest during the off-season months, though. I'd grow sweetbay magnolia for the fragrance alone, so in my book, all of these other features are just bonus points.

## PARROTIA: IT GROWS ON YOU

I should tell you first that my last pick isn't the best choice for gardeners looking for immediate gratification: Persian ironwood (*Parrotia persica*) doesn't grow all that quickly. But when it does start to mature, you'll know that this small- to medium-sized witch-hazel relative was worth the wait, as the trunk bark begins to flake off to reveal a camouflage-like mottling. Even before that, though, you'll enjoy seeing the small but abundant flowers, which bloom in a striking shade of deep cerise to burgundy along the smooth, gray, beech-like stems in early spring. And in fall, there's an incredible melody of foliage colors, shading from yellows and oranges all the way to burgundies. Persian ironwood isn't the easiest tree to find, but trust me, it's worth the hunt!

**Persian ironwood (*Parrotia persica*)**

# A Few More Favorites

You didn't really believe that I'd be able to stop at just 10 plants, did you? Here are a few more that I simply *couldn't* leave out of my favorites.

**'Purple Smoke' false indigo (*Baptisia*):** It's easy to think of baptisias as late-spring or early-summer perennials, but 'Purple Smoke' starts the show much earlier, with rich bronzy purple new growth that looks much like stout asparagus shoots rising from the ground. Flowering begins a few weeks after that, with a full month of smoky violet-and-purple bicolor blooms. Young plants may produce just one or two spikes, but be patient: We've counted as many as 50 bloom spikes on plants just three or four years old.

**'Purple Smoke' false indigo (*Baptisia*)**

'Gold Heart' bleeding heart (*Dicentra spectabilis*) with hosta

## 'Gold Heart' bleeding heart (*Dicentra spectabilis*):

Shocking chartreuse leaves with the classic pink-and-white bleeding-heart flower: what's not to love? I like to plant 'Gold Heart' with 'Queen of Night' tulips, so the bulbs' satiny purple-black flowers can pop up through its ferny greenish yellow foliage. Deer-proof and very reliable, 'Gold Heart' also tends to keep its leaves through the summer, long after the common bleeding heart has gone dormant. The only thing that would make this perennial better is if it had blue flowers!

## Dwarf Korean lilac (*Syringa meyeri* 'Palibin'):

I'm crazy about lilacs in general, but this one gets the nod for a few reasons. First, it flowers like crazy and starts about two weeks after common lilacs, so it's great for extending the lilac season. Dwarf Korean lilac also has a more refined appearance even when not in bloom. Unlike many lilacs, it has dependably good fall color, and it's resistant to powdery mildew, which often disfigures the leaves of the vulgaris types. It's also easier to fit the compact plants into a garden, and they tolerate hard pruning (right after flowering is finished) if you need to keep them even smaller.

Dwarf Korean lilac (*Syringa meyeri* 'Palibin') with 'Mon Amie' forget-me-nots (*Myosotis*)

CHAPTER 10

# THROUGH THE SEASONS

For many people, the new year begins on January 1. But for gardeners, it starts when the first new sprouts appear, making spring our time to celebrate a new cycle of life. It's the season for bulbs, early-flowering perennials, and even some trees and shrubs. As the weather warms up, so does the variety of flowers and foliage, culminating with a bounty of blooms and colorful leaves in fall. Even winter can be beautiful as berries, seedheads, and evergreens supply structure and create interest when silvered with frost or dusted with snow.

To help inspire you with ideas for your own garden, here's a gallery of some of our favorite plants and combinations through the seasons at Linden Hill Gardens.

## Early to Mid-Spring

Witch hazel (*Hamamelis* x *intermedia*) [mid-March]

'Carlton' daffodils (*Narcissus* hybrid) [late March]

**Above:** Golden creeping Jenny (*Lysimachia nummularia* 'Aurea'), Chocolate Chip ajuga (*Ajuga reptans* 'Valfredda'), and forget-me-nots (*Myosotis*) [late April]

**Right:** Fragrant winter hazel (*Corylopsis pauciflora*) [early April]

**Above:** 'Kingston Cardinal' Lenten Rose (*Helleborus* x *hybridus*) [mid-April]

**Below:** Hybrid columbines (*Aquilegia*) with forget-me-nots (*Myosotis*) and Chocolate Chip ajuga (*Ajuga reptans* 'Valfredda') [late April]

**Above:** 'Hearts of Gold' redbud (*Cercis canadensis*) [late April]

# Late Spring

**Above left:** Fingerleaf rodgersia (*Rodgersia aesculifolia*) with creeping mazus (*Mazus reptans*) and 'All Gold' Japanese wind grass (*Hakonechloa macra*) [early May]

**Above right:** Variegated sweet iris (*Iris pallida* 'Variegata') [mid-May]

**Right:** 'Ultramarine' forget-me-not (*Myosotis*) with 'Stairway to Heaven' Jacob's ladder (*Polemonium reptans*) and 'Inwersen's Variety' bigroot geranium (*Geranium macrorrhizum*) [mid-May]

**Below:** *Heuchera* 'Caramel' and Bowles' golden sedge (*Carex elata* 'Aurea') [late May]

**Above:** 'Ultramarine' forget-me-not (*Myosotis*) and golden creeping Jenny (*Lysimachia nummularia* 'Aurea') [mid-May]

**Below:** Camassia (*Camassia leitchlinii*) [mid-May]

# Early Summer

**Above:** 'Super Ego' Siberian iris (*Iris sibirica*) with Knock Out rose (*Rosa* 'Radrazz') [early June]

**Right:** *Salvia* 'Caradonna' and 'Anthea' yarrow (*Achillea*) [mid-June]

**Right:** Golden Spirit smoke bush (*Cotinus coggygria* 'Ancot') [mid-June]

**Below:** *Geranium* 'Johnson's Blue and ornamental onions (*Allium*) [late June]

81

# Midsummer

**Right:** 'Stella d'Oro' (*Hemerocallis*), 'Magnus' purple coneflower (*Echinacea purpurea*), Russian sage (*Perovskia*), and butterfly bush (*Buddleia*) [mid-July]

**Below:** 'Becky Towe' phlox (*Phlox paniculata*) with 'Silvery Sunproof' liriope (*Liriope muscari*), Rozanne geranium (*Geranium* 'Gerwat'), and 'Jester' purple millet (*Pennisetum glaucum*) [mid-July]

**Above, left:** 'Heaven-ly Blue' morning glory (*Ipomoea*) [mid-July]

**Above, right:** Love-lies-bleeding (*Ama-ranthus caudatus*) and 'Amora' coleus (*Solenostemon*) [late July]

**Left:** 'Purple Prince' zinnia (*Zinnia ele-gans*), Mellow Yellow spirea (*Spiraea thun-bergii* 'Ogon'), 'Ala-bama Sunset' coleus (*Solenostemon*), and 'Sweet Caroline Purple' sweet potato vine (*Ipomoea bata-tas*) [late July]

## Late Summer

**Above, left:** 'Black Knight' pincushion flower (*Scabiosa atropurpurea*), 'Gartenmeister Bonstedt' fuchsia (*Fuchsia triphylla*), and Mellow Yellow spirea (*Spiraea thunbergii* 'Ogon') [early August]

**Above, right:** Spanish flag (*Mina lobata*) [mid-August]

**Right:** Golden Spirit smoke bush (*Cotinus coggygria* 'Ancot') with coleus (*Solenostemon*) and 'Crackling Fire' million bells (*Calibrachoa*) [mid-August]

**Left:** 'Gateway' Joe-Pye weed (*Eupatorium purpureum*) with dwarf blue arctic willow (*Salix purpurea* 'Nana') [mid-August]

**Below, left:** 'Sedona' coleus (*Solenostemon*) with *Angelonia* 'Angelface Blue' [late August]

**Below, right:** *Gentiana triflora* var. *japonica* with 'Silvery Sunproof' liriope (*Liriope muscari*) [late August]

# Early Fall

**Above:** *Heuchera* 'Caramel' with Rozanne geranium (*Geranium* 'Gerwat') [early September]

**Right:** *Lobelia* 'Ruby Slippers' with variegated Japanese iris (*Iris ensata* 'Variegata') and 'Vivid' obedient plant (*Physostegia virginiana*) [early September]

**Above, left:** Blood banana (*Musa zebrina*) with variegated Japanese iris (*Iris ensata* 'Variegata') [mid-September]

**Above, right:** White African foxglove (*Ceratotheca triloba* 'Alba') with *Caryopteris* 'Snow Fairy', *Artemisia* 'Powis Castle', and *Browallia americana* [mid-September]

**Left:** Cardoon (*Cynara cardunculus*) with 'Little Bunny' fountain grass (*Pennisetum alopecuroides*) [late September]

# Mid- to Late Fall

**Right:** Variegated Japanese iris (*Iris ensata* 'Variegata'), 'Winter Red' winterberry (*Ilex verticillata)*, and Mexican bush sage (*Salvia leucantha*) [mid-October]

**Below, left:** *Salvia* 'May Night' with 'Baggesen's Gold' boxleaf honeysuckle (*Lonicera nitida*), *Cosmos* 'Cosmic Orange', and 'Lady in Red' Texas sage (*Salvia coccinea*) [mid-October]

**Below, right:** Mexican bush sage (*Salvia leucantha*) with *Chrysanthemum* 'Sheffield Pink' [mid-October]

**Left:** 'Redbor' kale with 'Golden Delicious' pineapple sage (*Salvia elegans*) [mid-October]

**Below:** 'Bluebird' smooth aster (*Aster laevis*) with lungwort (*Pulmonaria longifolia* subsp. *cevennensis*) [mid-October]

89

**Above, left:** Andean silver-leaf sage (*Salvia discolor*) [late October]

**Above, right:** Day-lily (*Hemerocallis*) with creeping bramble (*Rubus pentalobus*) [early November]

**Right:** *Chrysanthemum* 'Sheffield Pink' [late October]

# Winter

**Above, left:** 'Winter Red' winterberry (*Ilex verticillata*) [mid-December]

**Above, right:** 'Jelena' witch hazel (*Hamamelis* x *intermedia*) [mid-February]

**Left:** Purple coneflower (*Echinacea purpurea*) seedheads [mid-January]

# CHAPTER 11

# STONE IN THE GARDEN

Throughout my career as a landscape craftsman, I've often started the vision for my clients' gardens with the hardscape: walls, paths, patios, and the like. And in the majority of my designs, my hardscape material of choice is stone. From a practical standpoint, stone is much more durable and much less maintenance than wood. Wood, after all, eventually rots and needs to be replaced. Painting or staining may delay the process a few years, but that also increases the investment of time and money over the years. A properly constructed stone wall, path, or terrace, on the other hand, can last a lifetime.

Another reason that I like to use stone so much — and why I encourage others to use it as well — is its aesthetic appeal. This natural material complements all kinds of plantings, and its presence helps to link the garden to its setting in the larger landscape. In our part of Bucks County, we have a locally abundant igneous rock called diabase, which tends to appear in outcroppings of various-sized boulders. I sure wish people would take advantage of this great natural resource instead of buying in premade concrete building blocks, which look so harsh in the landscape.

In the spirit of encouraging gardeners to use whatever kind of stone they have access to, I'm sharing in this chapter some of the many ways that I've incorporated it into my work over the years. Some are traditional and familiar; others are somewhat quirky and unexpected. I'm not going to get into much how-to here, because there are plenty of great books on the subject, or you may choose to hire a professional mason for larger jobs. I just want to get you thinking about your design options. But I'll warn you now: stone can be very addictive. Once you do one project, you'll surely want more!

**Love those lichens.** Unlike most building materials, stone keeps getting better over the years, as it develops interesting patterns of lichens and mosses.

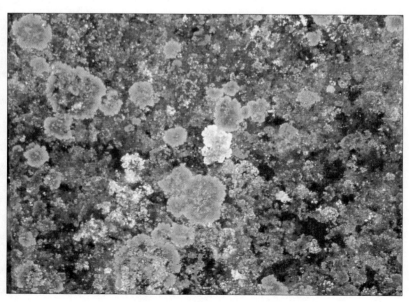

## WALLS

Walls, of course, are one of the most common uses for stone in the garden. In a sloping site, stone retaining walls set against the grade can terrace the area into flatter, more useful spaces. If a site is already flat, you can build stone walls and fill behind them with soil to create raised areas, or line excavated spaces with stone walls to develop a sunken garden. In any site, free-standing stone walls are a classic choice for creating boundaries and defining spaces within a garden. Special features such as curves, planted tops, or unique details within or atop the wall raise it to the level of garden art.

## WALKWAYS AND PATHS

I don't understand why builders and homeowners continue to create walkways by pouring boring concrete slabs and then sticking brick or flagstone on top as a veneer. In our cold-winter climate, the freezing temperatures cause the bricks or stones to break loose, and that requires regular repointing to put them back in place. There's a much simpler approach: excavate approximately 2 feet down, backfill with gravel, pack it firmly, and set in one or more large slabs of fieldstone or granite. The finished effect is more elegant, essentially maintenance-free, and often more cost-effective over the long run.

For secondary paths, pea gravel or crushed stone is often a good choice. It makes a nice scrunching sound underfoot, and it looks good, too. Plus, it's more environmentally friendly than a solid path, because it allows rainwater to drain through and soak into the soil instead of run off the site. Combining gravel with timbers or flagstones can help to keep the loose material in place. Installing gravel paths is a good way to spread out landscaping costs over time, as well: walk on them as they are for a few years, then use them as the base for stone slabs to create the permanent walkway as money allows.

# Getting Stoned

As you can probably tell by now, I love stone. I always have. As a young boy, I spent many hours with my father hunting stones in the woods on our property in northwest New Jersey and using them to craft unique projects. My stone obsession took a break when we moved to the coast of South Jersey: instead of boulders, we had only the yellow-orange pebbles gathered from local gravel pits and used for driveways and mulch. But when I moved to Pennsylvania to attend Delaware Valley College in Bucks County — a region filled with wonderful stone barns and farmhouses — my fascination with stone returned full force. Whenever I had the chance to explore, I would venture to local stone quarries and natural features such as High Rocks in Ralph Stove State Park and Haycock Mountain in Nockamixon State Park to study the local geology.

My dream of owning some fine Bucks County stonework came true when I bought the stone farmhouse and bank barn on the property now known as Linden Hill Gardens. I still enjoy studying rocks in natural setting and work stone into my design work any way I can. (In fact, one of my clients refers to me as "the boulder guy.") If you too love stone, I encourage you check out the web sites of two great organizations: The Stone Foundation (www.stonefoundation.org) and the Dry Stone Conservancy (www.drystone.org). They're must-see resources for anyone who appreciates the beauty of stone in buildings and landscapes.

## LIVING PATIOS

"Living patio" is a name I use for natural fieldstone slabs in a dry-pack (unmortared) setting, with spaces left between the stones for plants to grow in, bringing the whole setting to life. Check out Chapter 5, The Living Patio, for details on the design and construction of the living-patio feature here at Linden Hill Gardens.

## EDGINGS

Fieldstones set on edge make a study and handsome frame for raised beds. They also look great lining ground-level beds to keep the mulch and plants separate from adjacent lawn or gravel areas. Besides serving these practical purposes, stone edgings create a very strong visual element in the garden, especially in winter.

## FIRE PITS AND FIREPLACES

A stone-lined fire pit or stone fireplace is a great place to unwind after a long day at work, to eat a late dinner or simply to relax. These features are also popular with families looking for a space to hang out with friends and neighbors. You can build a lifetime of memories around the fireside while toasting marshmallows and telling stories!

## WATERFALLS AND FOUNTAINS

If you're planning a water feature for your garden, don't forget to incorporate stone. Use it to make the edging, to add height for a waterfall, or to form the base for a bubbling fountain element. Add a unique look to a pond by setting in large boulders with the tops as level as possible just above the water surface.

## BRIDGES

If you're lucky enough to have a stream run through your property, consider using a large stone slab to create a dramatic bridge to span it. Stone slabs can also be useful in wet, low-lying areas, providing a safe and sturdy point where you can cross on foot, with a tractor, or in a vehicle without getting stuck or creating ruts.

## BOWLS

When you're hunting for rocks, keep your eyes open for any that have natural depressions to hold water. Or, seek out natural rocks that have been carved to hold water. These features are beautiful in their own right, and birds and beneficial insects will appreciate the water source. Float a few flowers on the water for a pretty finishing touch for an outdoor party.

## BENCHES

A stone seat is very easy to construct, visually dramatic, and more cost-effective than a teak garden bench. If you aren't lucky enough to find a piece of stone perfectly shaped as a seat, as I did, take a fairly flat stone and lay it across two chunky logs for a rustic seat, or set it on two blocky base stones to create a permanent feature. I like to create a special sitting area by placing a stone bench in a space cut into a slope. It's especially nice when a site like this faces south, because the stone warms up quickly, making a cozy spot to sit from fall through spring. I've also designed stone chaise lounges with fragrant thyme plants around the edges to sit or lay on.

## MONOLITHS

Long, narrow stones look amazing when set on end and partially buried for support. A single standing stone makes a dramatic garden accent; a pair of stone posts emphatically marks an entrance or transition point. Where space allows, repeating the stones in lines, circles, or spirals creates a very powerful landscape feature. Or go all the way and build your own mini-Stonehenge: a landscape feature that's sure to get your neighbors talking!

# Making the Most of Stone

There's so much more to say about my favorite subject, but I'm just about out of space here, so I'll finish up with a few more pointers on finding and using stone in the garden.

***Keep it simple.*** While I encourage you to use lots of stone in your garden, I'll also recommend that you stick to just two or three kinds at most. Combining several different types and colors looks "busy" and can actually detract from the overall effect. A cut bluestone terrace and a fieldstone wall, for instance, could create an interesting contrast. But if you also added granite steps and a yellow-orange pea gravel paths—well, then, that gets to be a little *too much* contrast.

***Go local.*** I like to suggest sticking with the kind of stone that occurs naturally in areas within 10 miles or so of your home. Using native stone helps to focus your choices and ensures that your stone project will look natural and appropriate for your region. Plus, it can save you a bundle in shipping costs.

**Match, don't mix.** When adding new stone projects around an existing stone structure, matching the color range will help to visually tie the features together.

**Ask around.** You can save even more money on your projects by hunting for free sources of stone. It's sad to see old stone houses and barns being demolished for development, but you might be able to salvage some of the stone just for asking. The owner may be glad to give it to you rather than pay to have it hauled away. Another option is to spread the word among local farmers and builders that you're looking for stone. Quite often, people stop by our office to ask if we're interested in using the stone they've found when expanding their pastures or excavating for a new home. A third op-

**New life for old stone.** I'm all for restoring majestic old stone structures, as we did with the barn at Linden Hill. But if restoration simply isn't an option, then using that stone for other projects is a much better alternative than using it for fill.

tion is to ask landowners directly if they want to sell some of their rocks. Be careful about spending too much time eyeing up a property, though; I once approached a wary homeowner who was convinced that I had been watching her house with intentions of robbing her. She was amused when I finally convinced her I was just admiring her stone!

# CHAPTER 12

# WORKING WITH A DESIGNER

For many keen gardeners, the process of creating and nurturing their garden is just as important as the "finished product." For them, the idea of hiring someone to help with creating new garden spaces is almost inconceivable: why would you pay someone else to do the fun stuff? But there are also folks who would dearly love to enjoy a beautiful landscape but simply don't have the time, tools, confidence, or knowledge to do it themselves. And then there are those who like to plant and putter but need some help with the big picture, or with labor-intensive projects like bed-building and hardscaping. In my 20 years as a garden designer, I've enjoyed working with clients with a wide range of needs, budgets, and skill levels, and I've learned something about the entire design process from each one of them. In this chapter, I'd like to share some of my insights with you, so you'll know what to look for if you ever consider getting a professional's help with your own garden – or if you're a designer looking to improve your own business.

## FINDING THE RIGHT DESIGNER

As with hiring any professional, there are a number of ways to connect with a potential designer for your garden or landscaping project. You could go the research route, by looking in the telephone book, doing a web search, or visiting flower or home shows. If you see a garden or landscape you admire in your area, you could stop and ask the homeowner who did the design work. Or, you could ask friends, family, and fellow gardeners if they've worked with a designer that they really liked, or if they know of someone else who has.

Whichever type of design professional you choose to deal with, I suggest getting opinions from at least two of them. Have them come out to your property so you can meet them in person and get a sense of how they might be to work with, personality-wise. You want someone who is patient and who will listen to your ideas before telling you what *they* think you should do. They should also be willing to be flexible, and not just stick to their original idea if it isn't exactly what you want. It's almost inevitable that small issues and potential changes will come up along the way, and having a designer who's open to adjusting their plans will increase the chances of the project turning out the way you wish.

The next step should be to have a second meeting at a job that the designer has completed, so you can see his or her work for yourself. You'll get a good idea of the designer's abilities and style that way, and maybe even have the chance to speak with the homeowner about their own experience with the designer.

If you're more of a "let's get going" kind of person and don't want to go the second-opinion route, then I highly recommend starting the designer you've selected on a small job first. Once you see how the design proceeds and how the project turns out, you'll have a good idea as to whether you can trust them with a bigger area.

103

## THE DESIGN PROCESS

The actual steps involved in getting from concept to finished product can vary widely from designer to designer. Some will do a comprehensive site analysis and submit detailed plans and plant lists for your approval. Extensive up-front work like this gets factored into the cost of the project, but it gives you a measure of security, especially if you're working with a designer for the first time. Other designers will rely on a visual inspection of the site, tell you what they have in mind for plants and materials, and then pull everything together during the construction process. This requires a good deal of trust on your part, but it can be a very sensible, cost-saving approach when you're working with a designer who has plenty of practical experience, great design sense, and extensive plant knowledge. Either way, there are three points that most homeowners need to clarify up front: how much the project will cost, when it will start, and when it will be done.

**Getting Started.** My own design process as a landscape craftsman is rather different than that of many traditional designers, but it's an approach that's efficient and enjoyable for both me and my clients. It starts with an initial consultation at the client's home. I charge a fee for this session, which is deducted from the balance if the work is performed.

This meeting usually lasts 2 to 3 hours, during which time I listen to what the clients want, ask questions to get more details about their needs, and share my first impressions about the site and the possibilities. If they don't have specific ideas about what they want plant- or design-wise, I'll also toss out some more specific

**Out of ideas?** A designer can look at a site with fresh eyes and come up with a solution that's both beautiful and functional.

ideas about what could be done. Even "hands off" clients appreciate being involved in this initial brainstorming, because it makes us into a team, instead of me simply giving them what *I* think they should have. After all, they're the ones who have to live with the finished garden.

**Digging into Details.** Then, the homework starts. I ask the clients to mark pages of books and magazines that have pictures of plants, colors, structures, and design styles that they like, so I can get a more definite idea of their preferences. When they're ready, we set up a second meeting here at Linden Hill. During this session, which usually lasts about an hour, we review the materials they've marked, and I really get to know more about my clients as people. Sometimes I almost feel like a counselor when I'm working with couples: I find out that one loves purple foliage, while the other is crazy about variegated leaves, and they both hate chartreuse, for instance. My job is to find out what each one likes and dislikes and come up with suggestions that may satisfy both of them.

During this meeting, I start a running "plant menu" that I'll keep in their project folder. We usually begin the plant discussion indoors, but if time and the weather permit, we then head outside for a walk around the gardens here — especially our Deer-Resistant Garden, which highlights some of the best planting options for unfenced properties in our region. When homeowners can see in person what grows well around here, get ideas for interesting combinations, and actually smell and touch the plants too, the whole process gets even more exciting and "real" for them.

**The Final Step.** The last meeting before we start work is usually back at the client's site, where we go over the financial aspects of the project and walk through what we're thinking of for each area, plant- and design-wise. I don't do formal plans or sketches even for this part of the process. By this time, I feel like I really know the clients, and they've had plenty of opportunities to see the kinds of gardens I can create. Doing away with formal plans saves both of us time and money, and it avoids a whole lot of wasted paper and ink, too. Plus, it gets us on to the really fun part — actually digging in and getting the garden started — that much quicker!

# What's in a Name?

If you're a homeowner looking for help with siting plants or planting areas and perhaps some light construction (like pathways), you're probably looking for a *garden designer*. Garden designers are generally not certified and come from a wide range of backgrounds and experience levels.

The term *landscape designer* is often used interchangeably with garden designer. But there are landscape designers who belong to the Association of Professional Landscape Designers (APLD) and who have undergone a formal process to become a Certified Professional Landscape Designer. You can find out if there are any in your area through the APLD website (www.apld.com).

*Landscape contractors* usually concentrate on installing and maintaining gardens and landscapes, but they may provide design services as well.

A *landscape architect* has formal education in design, engineering, and construction — usually at the bachelor's or master's level — and usually must be licensed by the state(s) they work in. A landscape architect can be useful, or even a requirement, if your project will include more complex construction, such as retaining walls, terraces, outbuildings, drainage issues, or underground electric or irrigation lines. You can find a listing of these professionals through the American Society of Landscape Architects (www.asla.org).

# Let's Get Growing

Some designers maintain their own crews to do the actual construction and planting, while others coordinate with subcontractors or will help you connect with outside contractors to get the work done. Regardless of who does the work, remember that it's the homeowners' responsibility to arrange for any permits and inspections needed before or during the installation process.

***Timing is everything.*** If you can, try to schedule the installation of your garden for spring (in our part of Pennsylvania, mid-April to mid-June, before it gets hot, is ideal) or for fall (mid-September to mid-October, well before the ground freezes).

**Start with the soil.** Working perlite, compost, and other amendments into the soil ensures that the plants will get off to a great start.

***Don't skimp on soil preparation.*** I can't stress enough how important good soil prep is to the long-term success of any garden. My new design clients are often shocked when I explain that half or more of the total cost of their project can go into getting their site ready for planting! But they're always happy when they see the results in the following years, as their plants

thrive and fill out quickly to form a lush, healthy, beautiful garden.

***Be patient.*** Keep in mind that a newly planted garden needs some time to settle in and fill out. In good soil, spring-planted perennials can look great within a few months, while shrubs may take a full season or more to get established. Most trees need 1 year per caliper-inch of recovery time (about 3 years for a tree with a 3-inch-wide trunk, for example).

**Just wait!** New gardens, like the one at right, can look a little sparse at first, especially if you planted in fall or early spring. But you'll be amazed at how fast they'll fill out once the new growing season begins. Below is a different view of the same garden barely two months later.

*Artwork by Richard Van Duzer*

Linden Hill Gardens is open to the public from April through October. For hours and directions, please see our web site at www.lindenhillgardens.com.

We welcome garden clubs and other interested groups to visit our gardens and nursery. To arrange a tour, contact our office at 610-847-1300.

Jerry Fritz is available for speaking engagements and book signings. To arrange an event, contact our office at 610-847-1300.

LINDEN HILL GARDENS
8230 EASTON ROAD (ROUTE 611) P.O. BOX 10 OTTSVILLE, PA 18942

Made in the USA
Middletown, DE
25 November 2021

52612521R00062